JUMBLE®

BrainBusters!

A
Workout
for
Your Mind

David L. Hoyt and Russell L. Hoyt

TRIUMPH
BOOKS

This book is available at special discounts
for your group or organization.

For further information, contact:

Triumph Books
601 South LaSalle Street
Suite 500
Chicago, Illinois 60605
(312) 939-3330
FAX (312) 663-3557

ISBN 978-1-892049-28-5

Printed in the USA

CONTENTS

---

beginner puzzles

Jumble® BrainBusters #1 - #59

Page 1

---

intermediate puzzles

Jumble® BrainBusters #60 - #120

Page 61

---

advanced puzzles

Jumble® BrainBusters #121 - #177

Page 123

---

answers

Page 181

ANIMALS

Unscramble the Jumbles, one letter to each square, to spell names of animals.

#1 ROINH

#2 LEAEG

#3 KNSKU

#4 SMEUO

#5 LAWUSR

#6 ACCONOR

Box of Clues

Stumped? Maybe you can find a clue below. (No clue for the Mystery Answer.)

- Small rodent
- Sprayer
- Masked mammal
- Large bird of prey
- Heavyset herbivore
- Tusked mammal

Arrange the circled letters to solve the mystery answer.

MYSTERY ANSWER

TV SHOWS

Unscramble the Jumbles, one letter to each square, to spell names of TV shows.

#1 ATIX

#2 LAASLD

#3 EHECSR

#4 RSFAIRE

#5 CPITNIYS

#6 RTSATEKR

Box of Clues

Stumped? Maybe you can find a clue below.

-Think "outer space"
-Think "drivers"
-Think "Boston"
-Think "Texas"
-Think "Seattle"
-Think "#1 in the '90s"
-Think "Michael J. Fox"

Arrange the circled letters to solve the mystery answer.

MYSTERY ANSWER

FOOD

JUMBLE. BrainBusters!

Unscramble the Jumbles, one letter to each square, to spell words related to food.

#1 ZIPAZ
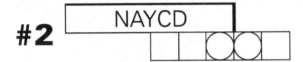

#2 NAYCD

#3 NODTU

#4 KIPELC

#5 EURBRG

#6 HEPTCKU

Interesting Food Facts

The number of burgers sold by McDonald's is more than 10 times the number of people on Earth.

Welch's developed its first jam in 1918.

General Mills introduced Trix cereal in 1954.

Arrange the circled letters to solve the mystery answer.

MYSTERY ANSWER

U.S. STATES

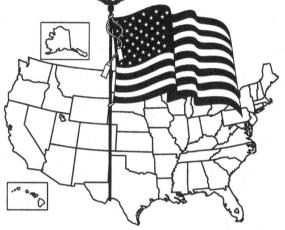

Unscramble the Jumbles, one letter to each square, to spell names of U.S. states.

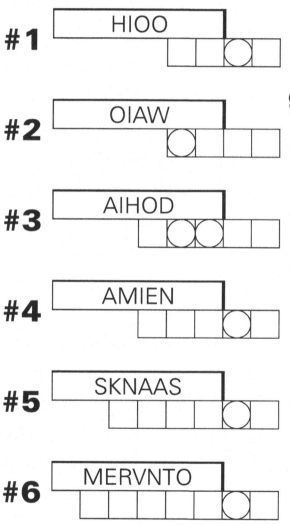

#1 HIOO

#2 OIAW

#3 AIHOD

#4 AMIEN

#5 SKNAAS

#6 MERVNTO

Arrange the circled letters to solve the mystery answer.

Interesting U.S. State Facts

New Jersey was named for the English Channel island of Jersey.

The name Kansas comes from the Sioux Indian word that most likely meant "people of the south wind."

The name Utah comes from a Navajo word meaning "higher up."

MYSTERY ANSWER

OUTER SPACE

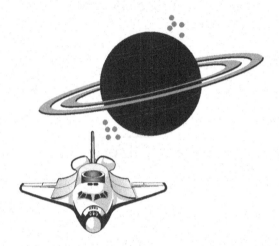

JUMBLE BrainBusters!

Unscramble the Jumbles, one letter to each square, to spell words related to outer space.

#1 ECOMT

#2 RSTNUA

#3 PELIECS

#4 AGITYRV

#5 EPNNTEU

#6 RERMYUC

Box of Clues

Stumped? Maybe you can find a clue below. (No clue for the Mystery Answer.)

-Attractive force
-Long-distance orbiter
-Solar _____
-Eighth planet
-Ringed planet
-Small, rocky planet

Arrange the circled letters to solve the mystery answer.

MYSTERY ANSWER

ALL ABOUT MONEY

Unscramble the Jumbles, one letter to each square, to spell words related to money.

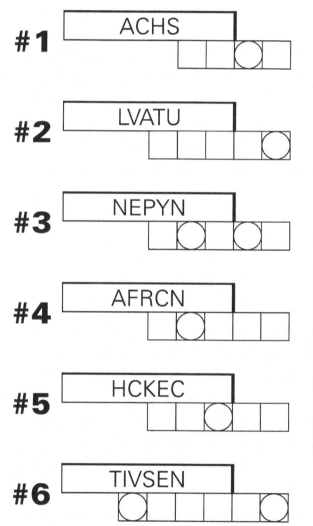

#1 ACHS

#2 LVATU

#3 NEPYN

#4 AFRCN

#5 HCKEC

#6 TIVSEN

Box of Clues

Stumped? Maybe you can find a clue below.

- Cent coin
- French currency
- Money
- Secure storage area
- Charge for money
- Written bank order
- Commit money for a profit

Arrange the circled letters to solve the mystery answer.

MYSTERY ANSWER

MOVIES

JUMBLE. BrainBusters!

Unscramble the Jumbles, one letter to each square, to spell titles of movies.

#1 ALNIE

#2 ARIZLB

#3 SCINOA

#4 OPTNTA

#5 YPCOSH

Box of Clues

Stumped? Maybe you can find a clue below.

- 1960 Hitchcock movie
- 1979 Sigourney Weaver sci-fi
- 1970 George C. Scott war movie
- 1942 romance
- 1985 Robert De Niro movie
- 1995 movie set in Las Vegas
- 1985 Harrison Ford movie

#6 TSWIESN

Arrange the circled letters to solve the mystery answer.

MYSTERY ANSWER

CLOTHING

Unscramble the Jumbles, one letter to each square, to spell words related to clothing.

#1 TSIHR

#2 LOGEV

#3 CJKTEA

#4 DNSALA

#5 TIMENT

#6 NAESERK

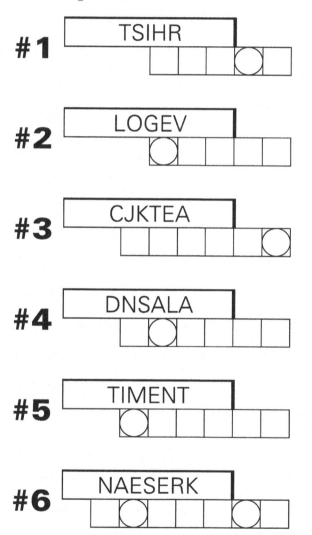

Box of Clues

Stumped? Maybe you can find a clue below. (No clue for the Mystery Answer.)

-Starts with "J"; ends with "T"
-Starts with "S"; ends with "T"
-Starts with "G"; ends with "E"
-Starts with "S"; ends with "R"
-Starts with "M"; ends with "N"
-Starts with "S"; ends with "L"

Arrange the circled letters to solve the mystery answer.

MYSTERY ANSWER

MEANS THE SAME

JUMBLE BrainBusters!

Unscramble the Jumbles, one letter to each square, to spell pairs of words with similar meanings.

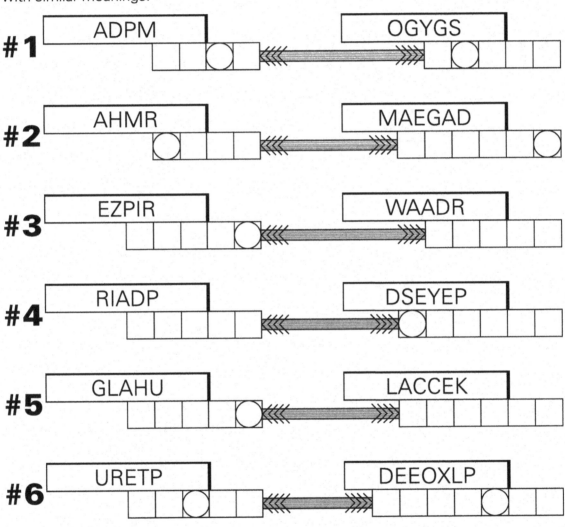

#1 ADPM — OGYGS

#2 AHMR — MAEGAD

#3 EZPIR — WAADR

#4 RIADP — DSEYEP

#5 GLAHU — LACCEK

#6 URETP — DEEOXLP

Arrange the circled letters to solve the mystery answer.
(Form two words with similar meanings.)

MYSTERY ANSWER

SHOPPING

Unscramble the Jumbles, one letter to each square, to spell words related to shopping.

#1 FIGT

#2 RCIPE

#3 LECKR

#4 SOERT

#5 POCUNO

#6 ORSBEW

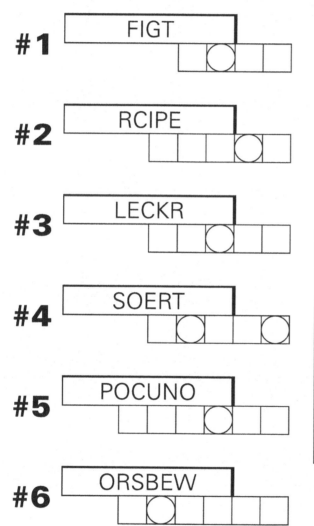

Box of Clues

Stumped? Maybe you can find a clue below.

- Attendant
- Cost
- Type of record
- Discount certificate
- Look around
- Present
- Shop, outlet

Arrange the circled letters to solve the mystery answer.

MYSTERY ANSWER

BASKETBALL

JUMBLE BrainBusters!

Unscramble the Jumbles, one letter to each square, to spell words related to basketball.

#1 LFOU

#2 TPIOV

#3 KLCBO

#4 BESATK

#5 EEFERER

#6 FEEDSEN

Interesting Basketball Facts

Spalding has estimated that an average NBA basketball has a life span of about 10,000 bounces.

The distance of the three-point line in the NBA is 22 feet.

A basketball hoop is 18 inches in diameter.

Arrange the circled letters to solve the mystery answer.

MYSTERY ANSWER

NEW ENGLAND

Unscramble the Jumbles, one letter
to each square, to spell words related
to New England.

#1 AIENM

#2 SOONTB

#3 LIGIMRP

#4 MOERTNV

#5 ECPODCA

#6 ROAHFTDR

Box of Clues

Stumped? Maybe you can find a clue
below.

-Largest New England state
-Green Mountain state
-Largest New England city
-Connecticut capital
-Smallest New England state
-Massachusetts peninsula
-New England settler

Arrange the circled letters
to solve the mystery answer.

MYSTERY ANSWER

AUTOMOBILES

Unscramble the Jumbles, one letter to each square, to spell words related to automobiles.

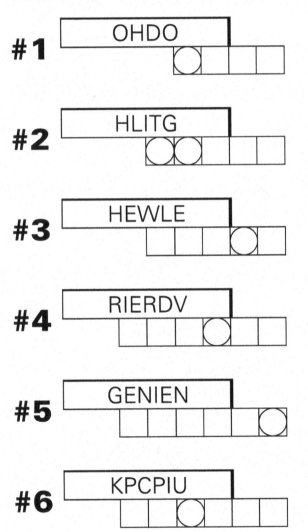

#1 OHDO

#2 HLITG

#3 HEWLE

#4 RIERDV

#5 GENIEN

#6 KPCPIU

Box of Clues

Stumped? Maybe you can find a clue below. (No clue for the Mystery Answer.)

-Starts with "E"; ends with "E"
-Starts with "W"; ends with "L"
-Starts with "P"; ends with "P"
-Starts with "D"; ends with "R"
-Starts with "L"; ends with "T"
-Starts with "H"; ends with "D"

Arrange the circled letters to solve the mystery answer.

MYSTERY ANSWER

NORTH AMERICA

Unscramble the Jumbles, one letter to each square, to spell words related to North America.

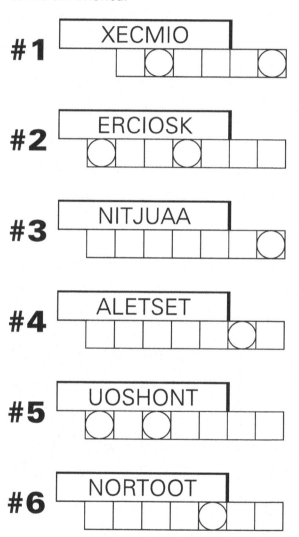

#1 XECMIO

#2 ERCIOSK

#3 NITJUAA

#4 ALETSET

#5 UOSHONT

#6 NORTOOT

Box of Clues

Stumped? Maybe you can find a clue below.

- Large Canadian city
- Third largest North American country
- Mountain chain
- Mexican city
- "Great" body
- Large Southern U.S. city
- Puget Sound city

Arrange the circled letters to solve the mystery answer.

MYSTERY ANSWER

HEALTH & FITNESS

JUMBLE
BrainBusters!

Unscramble the Jumbles, one letter to each square, to spell words related to health and fitness.

#1 RITNA

#2 TEIAGN

#3 LSMUEC

#4 NGRINNU

#5 BERAIOC

#6 TSTEHNGR

Box of Clues

Stumped? Maybe you can find a clue below. (No clue for the Mystery Answer.)

-Starts with "R"; ends with "G"

-Starts with "M"; ends with "E"

-Starts with "T"; ends with "N"

-Starts with "A"; ends with "C"

-Starts with "E"; ends with "G"

-Starts with "S"; ends with "H"

Arrange the circled letters to solve the mystery answer.

MYSTERY ANSWER

ELEMENTS

Unscramble the Jumbles, one letter to each square, to spell names of elements.

#1 ZCIN

#2 EPCROP

#3 ACLTBO

#4 USULFR

#5 HMUILE

#6 SLINICO

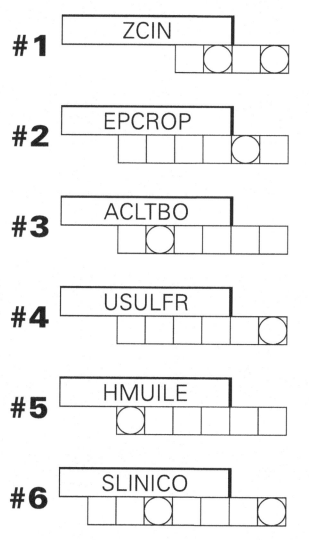

THE PERIODIC TABLE

Box of Clues

Stumped? Maybe you can find a clue below.

-Starts with "C"; ends with "R"
-Starts with "Z"; ends with "C"
-Starts with "C"; ends with "E"
-Starts with "H"; ends with "M"
-Starts with "C"; ends with "T"
-Starts with "S"; ends with "N"
-Starts with "S"; ends with "R"

Arrange the circled letters to solve the mystery answer.

MYSTERY ANSWER

THE HUMAN BODY

JUMBLE.
BrainBusters!

Unscramble the Jumbles, one letter to each square, to spell words related to the human body.

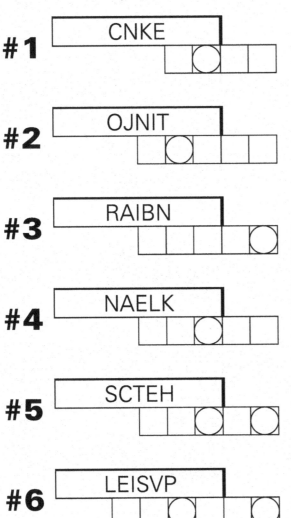

#1 CNKE

#2 OJNIT

#3 RAIBN

#4 NAELK

#5 SCTEH

#6 LEISVP

Interesting Human Body Facts

There are trillions of cells in the human body.

The thumbnail is the slowest growing part of the fingernails.

The brain uses up 20 percent of the human body's oxygen supply.

Arrange the circled letters to solve the mystery answer.

MYSTERY ANSWER

SPORTS

JUMBLE BrainBusters!

Unscramble the Jumbles, one letter to each square, to spell words related to sports.

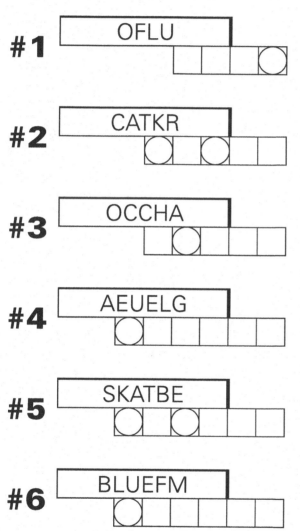

#1 OFLU

#2 CATKR

#3 OCCHA

#4 AEUELG

#5 SKATBE

#6 BLUEFM

Box of Clues

Stumped? Maybe you can find a clue below. (No clue for the Mystery Answer.)

-Starts with "F"; ends with "E"
-Starts with "C"; ends with "H"
-Starts with "F"; ends with "L"
-Starts with "L"; ends with "E"
-Starts with "T"; ends with "K"
-Starts with "B"; ends with "T"

Arrange the circled letters to solve the mystery answer.

MYSTERY ANSWER

ACTORS & ACTRESSES

JUMBLE. BrainBusters!

Unscramble the Jumbles, one letter to each square, to spell the names of actors and actresses.

#1 ERHRDISA

#2 MJICAYRER

#3 RDIMEOOEM

Box of Clues

Stumped? Maybe you can find a clue below.

-The Truman Show, The Cable Guy
-Three Men and a Baby
-Apollo 13, The Rock
-Ghost, Disclosure
-Edward Scissorhands, Donnie Brasco
-Heat, City Hall
-Foul Play, Shampoo

#4 YJHONENPPD

#5 AOLWDGIEHN

#6 COTSEMLEKL

Arrange the circled letters to solve the mystery answer.

MYSTERY ANSWER

COUNTRY FLAGS

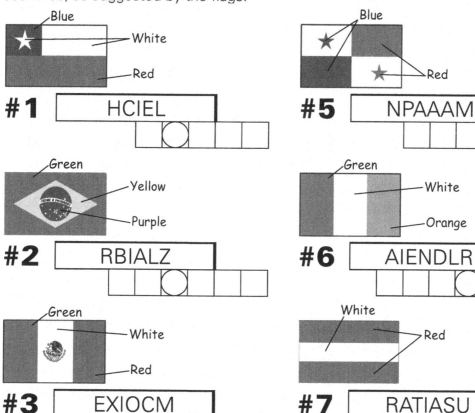

Unscramble the Jumbles, one letter to each square, to spell names of countries, as suggested by the flags.

#1 HCIEL

#2 RBIALZ

#3 EXIOCM

#4 WEENDS

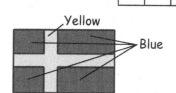

#5 NPAAAM

#6 AIENDLR

#7 RATIASU

Arrange the circled letters to solve the mystery answer.

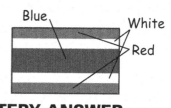

MYSTERY ANSWER

ALL ABOUT PLANTS

Unscramble the Jumbles, one letter to each square, to spell words related to plants.

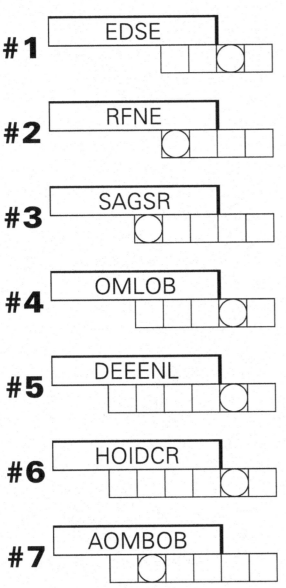

#1 EDSE

#2 RFNE

#3 SAGSR

#4 OMLOB

#5 DEEENL

#6 HOIDCR

#7 AOMBOB

Box of Clues

Stumped? Maybe you can find a clue below. (No clue for the Mystery Answer.)

-Plant with slender leaves
-Flower
-Stiff, pointed leaf
-Beginning
-Woody grass
-Three-petaled flower
-Spore producer

Arrange the circled letters to solve the mystery answer.

MYSTERY ANSWER

EUROPEAN COUNTRIES

Unscramble the Jumbles, one letter to each square, to spell names of European countries.

#1 CAERNF

#2 SNEEWD

#3 LAIERDN

#4 TUISAAR

#5 ANNEGDL

#6 LEUMGIB

Mystery Answer Facts

- Home to about 11 million
- Takes up about 50,000 square miles
- Its largest city is also its capital
- 75 percent of this country is mountainous
- Home to the Struma River

Arrange the circled letters to solve the mystery answer.

MYSTERY ANSWER

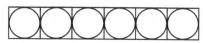

THE CIRCUS

JUMBLE BrainBusters!

Unscramble the Jumbles, one letter to each square, to spell words related to the circus.

#1 GIERT

#2 NOCNNA

#3 GULGRJE

Box of Clues

Stumped? Maybe you can find a clue below. (No clue for the Mystery Answer.)

-Starts with "J"; ends with "R"
-Starts with "C"; ends with "N"
-Starts with "T"; ends with "E"
-Starts with "T"; ends with "R"
-Starts with "A"; ends with "T"

#4 ZRAETEP

#5 RCOAATB

Arrange the circled letters to solve the mystery answer.

MYSTERY ANSWER

GOLF

Unscramble the Jumbles, one letter to each square, to spell words related to golf.

#1 SILEC

#2 HOGUR

#3 EOBYG

#4 GEEDW

#5 ERIRVD

#6 TUEPRT

Box of Clues

Stumped? Maybe you can find a clue below. (No clue for the Mystery Answer.)

-Lofted club
-Hook's opposite
-Green club
-Par + 1
-Longest club
-Tall grass

Arrange the circled letters to solve the mystery answer.

MYSTERY ANSWER

LARGE CITIES

JUMBLE BrainBusters!

Unscramble the Jumbles, one letter to each square, to spell the names of large cities.

#1 CAOIR

#2 REINLB

#3 DYSNYE

#4 DADRIM

#5 MOABYB

#6 OTROONT

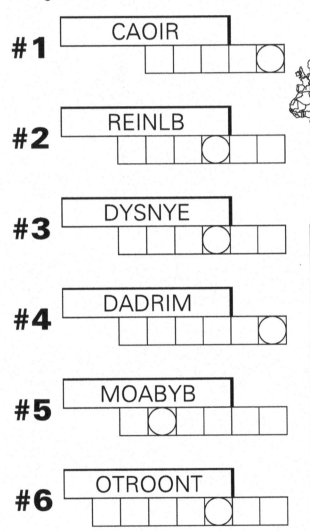

Box of Clues

Stumped? Maybe you can find a clue below. (No clue for the Mystery Answer.)

-Starts with "S"; ends with "Y"
-Starts with "B"; ends with "Y"
-Starts with "C"; ends with "O"
-Starts with "T"; ends with "O"
-Starts with "M"; ends with "D"
-Starts with "B"; ends with "N"

Arrange the circled letters to solve the mystery answer.

MYSTERY ANSWER

WEATHER

Unscramble the Jumbles, one letter to each square, to spell words related to weather.

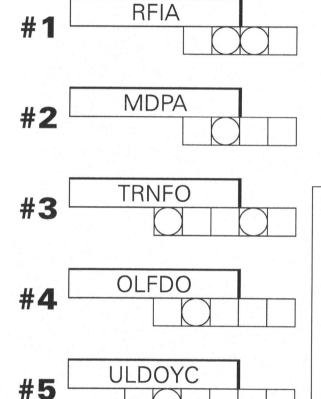

#1 RFIA

#2 MDPA

#3 TRNFO

#4 OLFDO

#5 ULDOYC

#6 ZRFEEE

Interesting Weather Facts

Stampede Pass, Wash., receives an average of more than 400 inches of snow a year. It is considered the snowiest city in the United States.

Oak Ridge, Tenn., is considered the least windy city in the U.S. with an average wind speed of just more than 4 mph.

Arrange the circled letters to solve the mystery answer.

MYSTERY ANSWER

MUSICAL INSTRUMENTS

JUMBLE BrainBusters!

Unscramble the Jumbles, one letter to each square, to spell names of musical instruments.

#1 AHPR

#2 LFUET

#3 NABOJ

#4 TUIRAG

#5 CIPOOCL

#6 ERUTPTM

Interesting Music Fact

Eric Clapton attended Kingston College of Art. He had planned on becoming a stained-glass designer, but changed his mind after he was expelled for playing his guitar in an art class. He then worked as a manual laborer, while practicing the guitar in his spare time.

Arrange the circled letters to solve the mystery answer.

MYSTERY ANSWER

PRESIDENTS

Unscramble the Jumbles, one letter to each square, to spell last names of U.S. presidents.

#1 OPKL

#2 EAHSY

#3 ARNGT

#4 MADSA

#5 OTCNNIL

#6 SJCAONK

Box of Clues

Stumped? Maybe you can find a clue below. (No clue for the Mystery Answer.)

- Civil War hero
- James _____
- Second or sixth
- Seventh president
- Rhodes scholar '68 -'70
- 19th president

Arrange the circled letters to solve the mystery answer.

MYSTERY ANSWER

HERBIVORES

JUMBLE BrainBusters!

Unscramble the Jumbles, one letter to each square, to spell herbivores.

#1 PHPIO

#2 LAMCE

#3 EZARB

#4 POEGRH

#5 FAIREFG

#6 FFAUOBL

#7 GRAKOOAN

Herbivore

Herbivore is the term commonly applied to any animal whose diet consists wholly or largely of plant material.

Arrange the circled letters to solve the mystery answer.

MYSTERY ANSWER

BIRDS

Unscramble the Jumbles, one letter to each square, to spell types of birds.

#1 AHKW

#2 RENW

#3 CWRO

#4 RSTKO

#5 GIPONE

#6 NACRYA

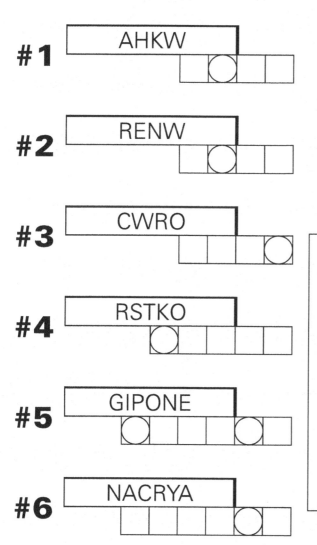

Interesting Bird Facts

Young birds must eat at least half their body weight in food each day to survive. This keeps the parents quite busy.

The smallest bird is the hummingbird. Some are so small that one of their enemies is the praying mantis.

Arrange the circled letters to solve the mystery answer.

MYSTERY ANSWER

FAMOUS ATHLETES

JUMBLE BrainBusters!

Unscramble the Jumbles, one letter to each square, to spell names of famous athletes.

#1 OHEW

#2 RBTET

#3 RERBA

#4 RBONW

#5 MTAHAN

#6 FIFGROD

Box of Clues

Stumped? Maybe you can find a clue below.

- Kansas City's George
- Football Jim
- Famous golfer
- New York's Joe
- Yankee catcher
- Hockey Gordie
- Football Frank

Arrange the circled letters to solve the mystery answer.

 **MYSTERY ANSWER**

PARTS OF AN AIRPLANE

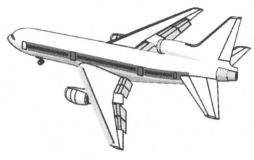

Unscramble the Jumbles, one letter to each square, to spell parts of an airplane.

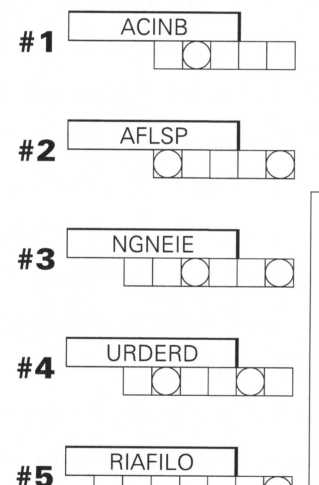

#1 ACINB

#2 AFLSP

#3 NGNEIE

#4 URDERD

#5 RIAFILO

Arrange the circled letters to solve the mystery answer.

Interesting Airplane Facts

The "D" and "C" in "DC-10" stand for Douglas Commercial.

The first aerial photograph taken from an airplane was taken in 1911.

The first commercial passenger airplane with a bathroom debuted in 1919.

MYSTERY ANSWER

THE HUMAN BODY

JUMBLE BrainBusters!

Unscramble the Jumbles, one letter to each square, to spell words related to the human body.

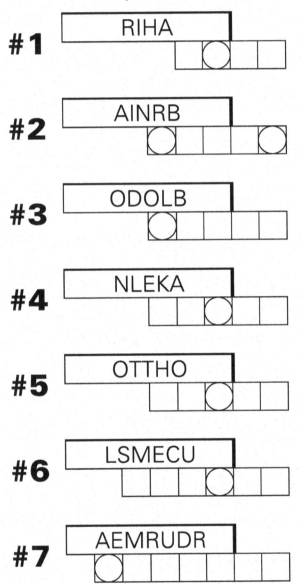

#1 RIHA

#2 AINRB

#3 ODOLB

#4 NLEKA

#5 OTTHO

#6 LSMECU

#7 AEMRUDR

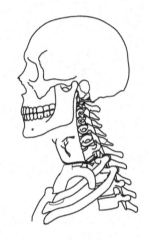

Box of Clues

Stumped? Maybe you can find a clue below. (No clue for the Mystery Answer.)

- -Important fluid
- -Lower joint
- -Control center
- -Follicle
- -Strong tissue
- -Bone-like outgrowth
- -Tympanic membrane

Arrange the circled letters to solve the mystery answer.

MYSTERY ANSWER

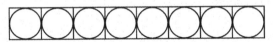

POETRY

JUMBLE BrainBusters!

Unscramble the Jumbles, one letter to each square, to spell words found in the poem.

#1 GTRHHUO

#2 EILCRNDH

#3 WTUNOP

#4 OLPPEE

#5 HEOM

#6 APPERA

#7 NIERTW

WINTER'S ARRIVAL
by Kim Nolan

A blustery wind blows
All _____ #1 our town
_____ #2 look up
As snow falls down

_____ #3 and downtown
_____ #4 begin to scurry
They rush to get _____ #5
It's beginning to flurry

Sidewalks get shoveled
Snow plows _____ #6
Get out your parkas
_____ #7 is here

Arrange the circled letters
to solve the mystery answer.
(The mystery answer is not
in the poem.)

MYSTERY ANSWER

SCHOOL

JUMBLE BrainBusters!

Unscramble the Jumbles, one letter to each square, to spell words related to school.

#1 ETTS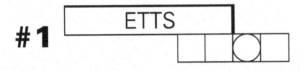

#2 RAYTD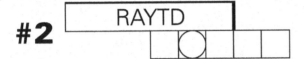

#3 LEEXP

#4 NULHC

#5 WASREN

#6 CCIEENS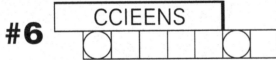

★ **JUMBLE® Trivia** Quick Quiz

Where might you be if you were at a school founded in 1636?

ARHVADR

ANSWER:

Arrange the circled letters to solve the mystery answer.

MYSTERY ANSWER

MATH

JUMBLE BrainBusters!

Unscramble the Jumbled letters, one letter to each square, so that each equation is correct.

For example: NOLSOEPNEU
ONE PLUS ONE = TWO

#1 WSXTXSVIELIE

◻◻◯◻ + ◻◯◻◻ = ◻◯◻◻◻◻

#2 OWEOFTTIUHRG

◻◻◯◻ × ◻◯◻◻ = ◻◯◻◻◻

#3 EVFOOENNIEEENVS

◯◻◻◻◻ + ◯◻◻◻ + ◻◯◻ = ◻◻◻◯◻◻

#4 FVTETLOWUEERREH

◯◻◻◻◻◻ ÷ ◻◻◯◻ = ◻◻◯◻◻◻

#5 WOOTFRTRHEUWOOT

◯◻◻ + ◻◯◻◻ = ◻◻◻◻◻◯ × ◯◻◻◻

Then arrange the circled letters to solve the mystery equation.

MYSTERY EQUATION

◯◯◯ × ◯◯◯ = ◯◯◯◯◯◯◯ ÷ ◯◯◯◯

FLORIDA

JUMBLE BrainBusters!

Unscramble the Jumbles, one letter to each square, to spell words related to Florida.

#1 CEHAB

#2 AAPTM

#3 MIMIA

#4 GRAOEN

#5 DRAOONL

#6 HNSNEISU

Box of Clues

Stumped? Maybe you can find a clue below.

-Florida export
-Florida formation
-Warm, light source
-Central Florida city
-Shoreline
-West Coast city
-South Florida city

Arrange the circled letters to solve the mystery answer.

MYSTERY ANSWER

SPORTS

JUMBLE BrainBusters!

Unscramble the Jumbles, one letter to each square, to spell words related to sports.

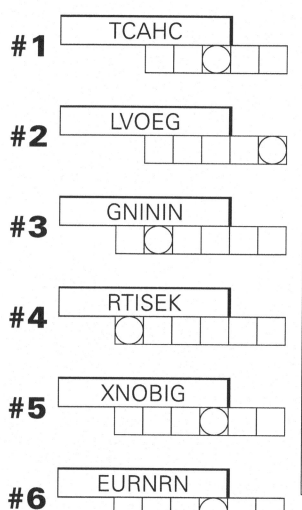

#1 TCAHC

#2 LVOEG

#3 GNININ

#4 RTISEK

#5 XNOBIG

#6 EURNRN

Interesting Sports Facts

The first basketball rule book was published in the late 1800s.

The New York Yankees were the first team to travel to a game via airplane.

A croquet ball weighs 1 pound.

Arrange the circled letters to solve the mystery answer.

MYSTERY ANSWER

FOOD

JUMBLE. BrainBusters!

Unscramble the Jumbles, one letter to each square, to spell words related to food.

#1 GESG

#2 LPEPA

#3 EHRCYR

#4 OTPTOA

#5 FUMINF

#6 AFWLEF

★ **JUMBLE® Trivia** Quick Quiz

What would you be eating if you were eating America's best-selling snack food?

TPPSTOHOAIC

ANSWER: ☐☐☐☐☐☐☐ ☐☐☐☐☐

Arrange the circled letters to solve the mystery answer.

MYSTERY ANSWER

⊙⊙⊙⊙⊙⊙⊙⊙⊙⊙

AROUND THE HOME

Unscramble the Jumbles, one letter to each square, to spell words related to the home.

#1 AWLL

#2 GITLH

#3 RCIAH

#4 ORFOL

#5 TUEOTL

#6 LEICIGN

Box of Clues

Stumped? Maybe you can find a clue below. (No clue for the Mystery Answer.)

-Room bottom
-Piece of furniture
-Room side
-Lamp
-Room top
-Electrical _____

Arrange the circled letters to solve the mystery answer.

MYSTERY ANSWER

U.S. STATE CAPITALS

Unscramble the Jumbles, one letter to each square, to spell names of U.S. state capitals.

#1 OBIES

#2 LAAYNB

#3 LNAISNG

#4 NHPOIXE

#5 AALTNAT

#6 AJOSNCK

Box of Clues

Stumped? Maybe you can find a clue below. (No clue for the Mystery Answer.)

-New York's capital
-Mississippi capital
-Idaho's capital
-Georgia's capital
-Arizona's capital
-Michigan's capital

Arrange the circled letters to solve the mystery answer.

MYSTERY ANSWER

OCCUPATIONS

Unscramble the Jumbles, one letter
to each square, to spell occupations.

#1 TIPLO

#2 HUTARO

#3 RAERBB

#4 ODTCRO

#5 TANJIRO

#6 MLUPERB

Box of Clues

Stumped? Maybe you can find a clue
below. (No clue for the Mystery Answer.)

-Starts with "D"; ends with "R"
-Starts with "J"; ends with "R"
-Starts with "A"; ends with "R"
-Starts with "B"; ends with "R"
-Starts with "P"; ends with "R"
-Starts with "P"; ends with "T"

Arrange the circled letters
to solve the mystery answer.

MYSTERY ANSWER

EUROPEAN CITIES

JUMBLE BrainBusters!

Unscramble the Jumbles, one letter to each square, to spell names of European cities.

#1 NBDLIU

#2 OONNDL

#3 SLIBNO

#4 DDRMIA

#5 NVINAE

#6 SWAAWR

Arrange the circled letters to solve the mystery answer.

MYSTERY ANSWER

ALL ABOUT MUSIC

JUMBLE BrainBusters!

Unscramble the Jumbles, one letter to each square, to spell words related to music.

#1 BOEO

#2 NPIOA

#3 RHOCD

#4 JAROM

#5 PETOM

#6 AUGIRT

Interesting Music Facts

In 1971, Barry Manilow produced Bette Midler's first big album entitled "The Divine Miss M."

It cost just $4 a ticket to see the Beatles when they played the Las Vegas Convention Center in 1964.

Arrange the circled letters to solve the mystery answer.

MYSTERY ANSWER

WEATHER

Unscramble the Jumbles, one letter to each square, to spell words related to weather.

JUMBLE
BrainBusters!

#1 SSHUL

#2 DLOFO

#3 DHUIM

#4 NDIYW

#5 MOTRS

#6 GEEDER

#7 RTIEWTS

Box of Clues

Stumped? Maybe you can find a clue below. (No clue for the Mystery Answer.)

-Unit
-Moist
-Violent storm
-Wintry mess
-Reason to find high ground
-Disturbance
-Blustery

Arrange the circled letters to solve the mystery answer.

MYSTERY ANSWER

COUNTRIES

Unscramble the Jumbles, one letter to each square, to spell names of countries.

#1 DINIA

#2 RUTEYK

#3 NIELCDA

#4 NFILNDA

#5 AHGNRYU

#6 MRAOIAN

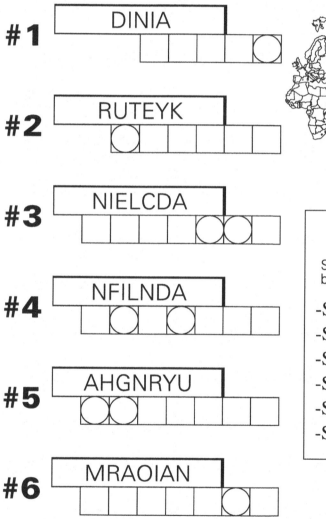

Box of Clues

Stumped? Maybe you can find a clue below. (No clue for the Mystery Answer.)

-Starts with "I"; ends with "D"

-Starts with "F"; ends with "D"

-Starts with "T"; ends with "Y"

-Starts with "R"; ends with "A"

-Starts with "I"; ends with "A"

-Starts with "H"; ends with "Y"

Arrange the circled letters to solve the mystery answer.

MYSTERY ANSWER

PLANET EARTH

JUMBLE BrainBusters!

Unscramble the Jumbles, one letter to each square, to spell words related to planet Earth.

#1 EIRRV

#2 CAEHB

#3 RCTSU

#4 PWASM

#5 NAILDS

#6 RYEEGS

Box of Clues

Stumped? Maybe you can find a clue below. (No clue for the Mystery Answer.)

-Everglades
-Shoreline
-Land drain
-Surface
-Watery vent
-Surrounded body

Arrange the circled letters to solve the mystery answer.

MYSTERY ANSWER

ABRAHAM LINCOLN

Unscramble the Jumbles, one letter to each square, to spell words related to Abraham Lincoln.

#1 AIRLP

#2 ACINB

#3 CSEHEP

#4 LWYARE

#5 ADBEET

#6 TKNUEKCY

Box of Clues

Stumped? Maybe you can find a clue below.

- Lincoln's birth state
- Lincoln-Douglas discussion
- Lincoln was born in one
- The Gettysburg Address, for example
- Lincoln title
- Month of Lincoln's death
- Lincoln left politics to become one in 1849

Arrange the circled letters to solve the mystery answer.

MYSTERY ANSWER

BIRDS

JUMBLE BrainBusters!

Unscramble the Jumbles, one letter to each square, to spell types of birds.

#1 ORNIB

#2 LGEEA

#3 KTROS

#4 EINPUNG

#5 CEPOAKC

#6 UZBRDZA

Box of Clues

Stumped? Maybe you can find a clue below.

- Golden _____
- Crested finch
- Southern bird
- Bird famous for its tail feathers
- Circling bird of prey
- Small thrush
- Large wading bird

Arrange the circled letters to solve the mystery answer.

MYSTERY ANSWER

ELEMENTS

JUMBLE BrainBusters!

Unscramble the Jumbles, one letter to each square, to spell names of elements.

#1 NRIO

#2 ULURFS

#3 TBCOAL

#4 LEIMUH

#5 CILSINO

#6 CMRUEYR

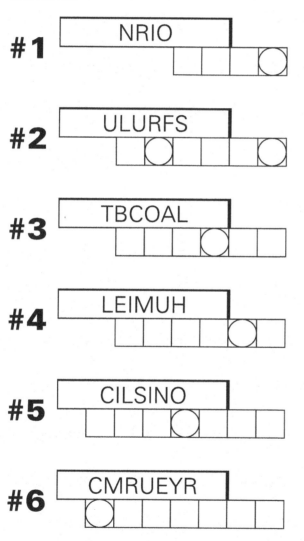

THE PERIODIC TABLE

Box of Clues

Stumped? Maybe you can find a clue below.

- Starts with "U"; ends with "M"
- Starts with "C"; ends with "T"
- Starts with "S"; ends with "R"
- Starts with "H"; ends with "M"
- Starts with "S"; ends with "N"
- Starts with "I"; ends with "N"
- Starts with "M"; ends with "Y"

Arrange the circled letters to solve the mystery answer.

MYSTERY ANSWER

AROUND THE HOME

Unscramble the Jumbles, one letter
to each square, to spell words related
to the home.

#1 RIBKC

#2 CIARH

#3 BAETL

#4 PEONH

#5 ORHCP

#6 RCAETP

Interesting Home Facts

The numbering of houses began
in Paris in the 1400s.
Numbering houses began in
England in the early 1700s.

The White House was designed
by architect James Horan in
1792.

The White House has more than
30 bathrooms.

Arrange the circled letters
to solve the mystery answer.

MYSTERY ANSWER

CLOTHING

Unscramble the Jumbles, one letter to each square, to spell words related to clothing.

#1 TOBO

#2 RAAKP

#3 BAIFCR

#4 TOIUTF

#5 UOBTNT

#6 MTIENT

Arrange the circled letters to solve the mystery answer.

Interesting Clothing Facts

Almost 50 percent of Americans own at least one piece of clothing with a professional sports team's logo on it.

Harry Truman worked at a clothing store before becoming president of the United States.

MYSTERY ANSWER

FOOD

JUMBLE BrainBusters!

Unscramble the Jumbles, one letter to each square, to spell words related to food.

#1 EFBE

#2 KANCS

#3 KOICEO

#4 LAFWEF

#5 TREPELZ

#6 EOAALMT

Interesting Food Facts

North Carolina's official state beverage is milk.

Because it was so much less expensive than sugar, molasses was the primary sweetener used in America until the 1920s.

Nearly all of the green olives grown in Italy are turned into olive oil.

Arrange the circled letters to solve the mystery answer.

MYSTERY ANSWER

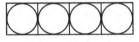
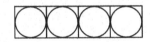

SPORTS

Unscramble the Jumbles, one letter to each square, to spell words related to sports.

#1 TUTPRE

#2 ORHYPT

#3 FAEDET

#4 AESNOS

#5 NCEIFGN

#6 RAHRYEC

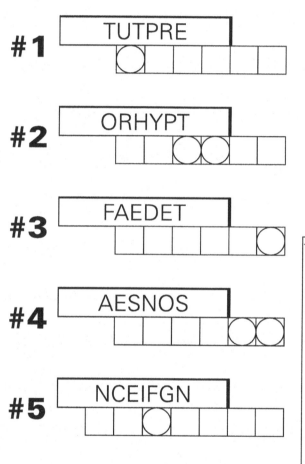

★ **JUMBLE® Trivia** Quick Quiz

What fast-paced sport might you be playing, if you were playing a sport that became an official Olympic event in 1992?

NABTMIDNO

ANSWER:

Arrange the circled letters to solve the mystery answer.

MYSTERY ANSWER

U.S. STATE CAPITALS

Unscramble the Jumbles, one letter to each square, to spell names of U.S. state capitals.

#1 SUIANT

#2 NEHLAE

#3 OSBONT

#4 LAREGIH

#5 TUAGSAU

#6 RCNOODC

Box of Clues

Stumped? Maybe you can find a clue in these Jumbled clues.
(No clue for the Mystery Answer.)

-Starts with "A"; ends with "A"
-Starts with "C"; ends with "D"
-Starts with "H"; ends with "A"
-Starts with "A"; ends with "N"
-Starts with "B"; ends with "N"
-Starts with "R"; ends with "H"

Arrange the circled letters to solve the mystery answer.

MYSTERY ANSWER

THE HUMAN BODY

JUMBLE. BrainBusters!

Unscramble the Jumbles, one letter to each square, to spell words related to the human body.

#1 UGLN

#2 EHDA

#3 OONCL

#4 OOTHT

#5 TUBMH

#6 AHRTOT

Box of Clues

Stumped? Maybe you can find a clue below.
(No clue for the Mystery Answer.)

- Brain area
- Intestine part
- Part of the neck
- One of two in the chest
- Hand part
- Molar, for example

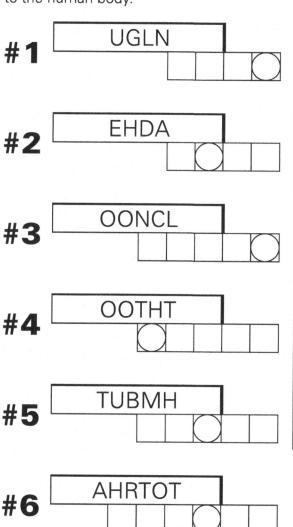

Arrange the circled letters to solve the mystery answer.

MYSTERY ANSWER

CANADA

Unscramble the Jumbles, one letter to each square, to spell words related to Canada.

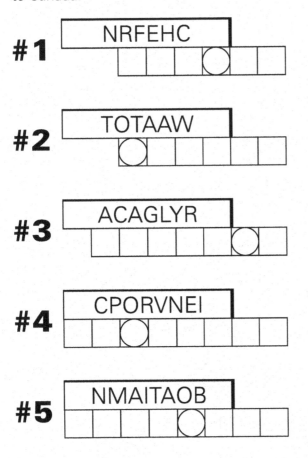

#1 NRFEHC

#2 TOTAAW

#3 ACAGLYR

#4 CPORVNEI

#5 NMAITAOB

#6 MTNORALE

Box of Clues

Stumped? Maybe you can find a clue below. (No clue for the Mystery Answer.)

- Eastern language
- Capital
- Home to Edmonton
- Nova Scotia, for example
- Home to Winnipeg
- Large Quebec city

Arrange the circled letters to solve the mystery answer.

MYSTERY ANSWER

AMERICAN INDIANS

Unscramble the Jumbles, one letter to each square, to spell names of American Indian tribes.

#1 KRECE

#2 BUOELP

#3 VOJMEA

#4 WOMAKH

#5 MEIOLENS

#6 HCEENENY

Box of Clues

Stumped? Maybe you can find a clue below.

-Starts with "M"; ends with "K"
-Starts with "C"; ends with "E"
-Starts with "P"; ends with "O"
-Starts with "M"; ends with "E"
-Starts with "C"; ends with "K"
-Starts with "C"; ends with "E"
-Starts with "S"; ends with "E"

Arrange the circled letters to solve the mystery answer.

MYSTERY ANSWER

MOVIES

JUMBLE BrainBusters!

Unscramble the Jumbles, one letter to each square, to spell titles of movies.

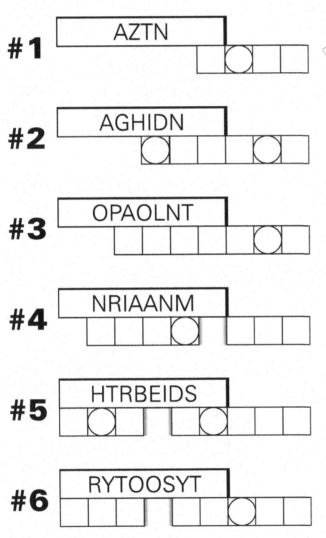

#1 AZTN

#2 AGHIDN

#3 OPAOLNT

#4 NRIAANM

#5 HTRBEIDS

#6 RYTOOSYT

Box of Clues

Stumped? Maybe you can find a clue below.

- 1963 Hitchcock movie
- 1998 Woody Allen (voice only) movie
- 1982 "Best Picture" Oscar winner
- 1952 Western
- 1995 Tom Hanks (voice only) movie
- 1986 "Best Picture" Oscar winner
- 1988 Hoffman, Cruise movie

Arrange the circled letters to solve the mystery answer.

MYSTERY ANSWER

FAMOUS ATHLETES

JUMBLE
BrainBusters!

Unscramble the Jumbles, one letter to each square, to spell names of famous athletes.

#1 OBGR

#2 SOLIU

#3 EBHNC

#4 TAYPNO

#5 RJONAD

#6 RFANOEM

Box of Clues

Stumped? Maybe you can find a clue below.

- Boxing Joe
- Dribbling Michael
- Scandinavian tennis player
- Catching Johnny
- Indiana shooter
- Running Walter
- Boxing (or grilling) George

Arrange the circled letters to solve the mystery answer.

MYSTERY ANSWER

OUTER SPACE

Unscramble the Jumbles, one letter to each square, to spell words related to outer space.

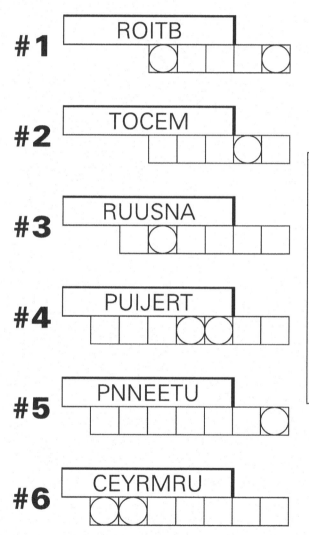

#1 ROITB

#2 TOCEM

#3 RUUSNA

#4 PUIJERT

#5 PNNEETU

#6 CEYRMRU

Arrange the circled letters to solve the mystery answer.

★ JUMBLE® Trivia Quick Quiz

What would you be eating, if you were eating what John Glenn ate when he had the first meal in space?

PAAESULECP

ANSWER:

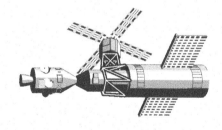

MYSTERY ANSWER

ALL ABOUT MONEY

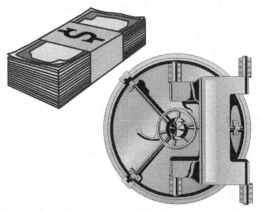

Unscramble the Jumbles, one letter to each square, to spell words related to money.

#1 TIMN

#2 UAVEL

#3 TSOKC

#4 UOPDN

#5 RCAEHG

#6 LOLRDA

Box of Clues

Stumped? Maybe you can find a clue below.

-Worth
-U.S. currency
-_____ certificate
-Written record
-Make out of metal
-British currency
-Pay later

Arrange the circled letters to solve the mystery answer.

MYSTERY ANSWER

THE HUMAN BODY

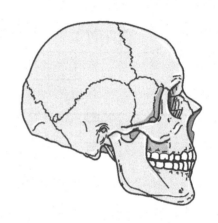

JUMBLE
BrainBusters!

Unscramble the Jumbles, one letter to each square, to spell words related to the human body.

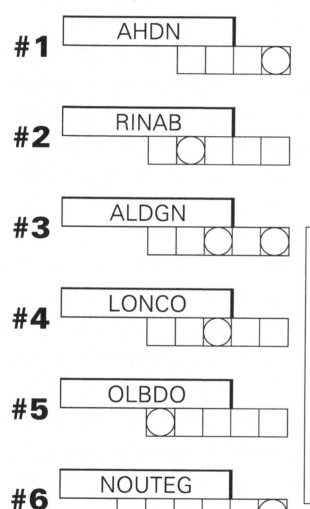

#1 AHDN

#2 RINAB

#3 ALDGN

#4 LONCO

#5 OLBDO

#6 NOUTEG

Interesting Human Body Facts

The human brain reaches its maximum weight at about age 20 (approx. 3 pounds).

The white part of the fingernail is the lunula.

The human hand contains thousands of nerve endings.

Arrange the circled letters to solve the mystery answer.

MYSTERY ANSWER

MAKING MOVIES

JUMBLE. BrainBusters!

Unscramble the Jumbles, one letter to each square, to spell words related to making movies.

#1 RPPO

#2 TNSTU

#3 RPSICT

#4 DTIOUS

#5 RIWTRE

#6 MARCAE

★ **JUMBLE® Trivia** Quick Quiz

What movie would you be watching if you were watching the 1964 "Best Picture" Oscar winner?

MLIAYARFYD

ANSWER:

Arrange the circled letters to solve the mystery answer.

MYSTERY ANSWER

AUTOMOBILES

Unscramble the Jumbles, one letter to each square, to spell words related to automobiles.

#1 AIORD

#2 URTKN

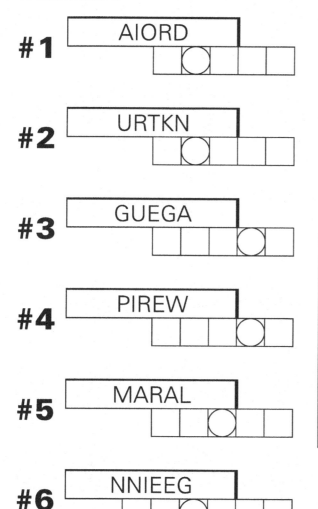

#3 GUEGA

#4 PIREW

Box of Clues

Stumped? Maybe you can find a clue below. (No clue for the Mystery Answer.)

- Water mover
- Car receiver
- Protective system
- Storage area
- An odometer, for example
- Power source

#5 MARAL

#6 NNIEEG

Arrange the circled letters to solve the mystery answer.

MYSTERY ANSWER

ANIMALS

JUMBLE® BrainBusters!

Unscramble the Jumbles, one letter to each square, to spell names of animals.

#1 DPAAN

#2 MICPH

#3 RTUTEL

#4 OCTEOY

#5 POEGRH

#6 UUVTERL

Interesting Animal Facts

There is a type of bat called a microbat. This type of bat weighs less than one ounce.

There is a type of earthworm in Australia that can grow to more than 10 feet in length.

More than 10,000 puppies are born in the U.S. every hour.

Arrange the circled letters to solve the mystery answer.

MYSTERY ANSWER

CLOTHING & FASHION

Unscramble the Jumbles, one letter to each square, to spell words related to clothing and fashion.

#1 SKCO

#2 TLESY

#3 LAITRO

#4 BAIFCR

#5 EVETVL

#6 BTOUNT

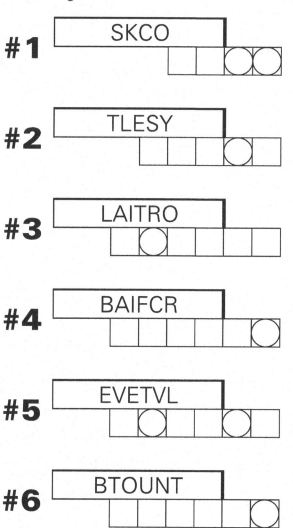

Interesting Fashion Facts

Michael Jordan has his shirts tailored to fit his 17 ½-inch neck, 40-inch sleeve, and 39 ½ -inch shirttail.

Fashion model Christie Brinkley sold ice cream before becoming a model.

Arrange the circled letters to solve the mystery answer.

MYSTERY ANSWER

BASEBALL

JUMBLE
BrainBusters!

Unscramble the Jumbles, one letter to each square, to spell words related to baseball.

#1 ACOHC

#2 TPRIEL

#3 GILNES

#4 DBOUEL

#5 WKALDE

#6 CACERHT

★ **JUMBLE® Trivia** Quick Quiz

Who would you have been talking to, if you had talked to the legendary sportscaster who handled the commentary for the first televised baseball game in 1939?

REREABRDB

ANSWER:

Arrange the circled letters to solve the mystery answer.

MYSTERY ANSWER

MEANS THE OPPOSITE

JUMBLE BrainBusters!

Unscramble the Jumbles, one letter
to each square, to spell pairs of words
with opposite meanings.

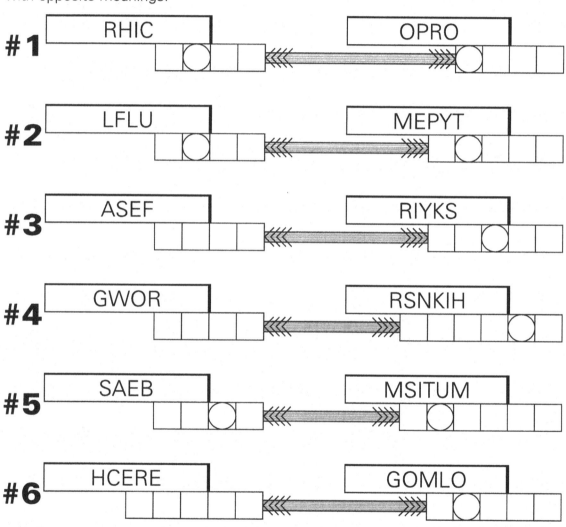

#1 RHIC — OPRO

#2 LFLU — MEPYT

#3 ASEF — RIYKS

#4 GWOR — RSNKIH

#5 SAEB — MSITUM

#6 HCERE — GOMLO

Arrange the circled letters to solve the mystery answer.
(Form two words with opposite meanings.)

MYSTERY ANSWER

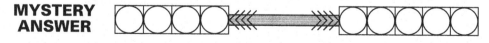

GOING TO THE DOCTOR

**JUMBLE.
BrainBusters!**

Unscramble the Jumbles, one letter
to each square, to spell words related
to going to the doctor.

#1 SKIC

#2 UCER

#3 CINICL

#4 TEAHHL

#5 GRSENOU

#6 SAHTOILP

Interesting Medical Facts

Approximately 25 percent of
prescription medicines in the
United States are derived from
plants.

Hippocrates, (the "Father of
Medicine") practiced medicine
in 400 B.C.

Arrange the circled letters
to solve the mystery answer.

MYSTERY ANSWER

PRESIDENTS

JUMBLE. BrainBusters!

Unscramble the Jumbles, one letter to each square, to spell last names of U.S. presidents.

#1 TFTA

#2 OFDR

#3 NNIXO

#4 VOREOH

#5 SWINOL

#6 OSJNNHO

Arrange the circled letters to solve the mystery answer.

★ **JUMBLE® Trivia** Quick Quiz

Who would you be talking to, if you were talking to the captain who signed Maj. Clark Gable's Army discharge papers?

NOALAGNREARD

ANSWER:

MYSTERY ANSWER

ALL ABOUT MUSIC

JUMBLE BrainBusters!

Unscramble the Jumbles, one letter to each square, to spell words related to music.

#1 ULFET

#2 NIVOIL

#3 NFILEA

#4 AUGIRT

#5 MTHYRH

#6 LEMDOY

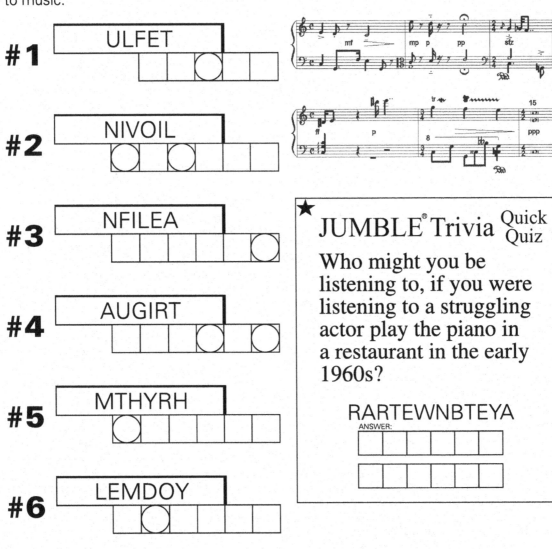

★ JUMBLE® Trivia Quick Quiz

Who might you be listening to, if you were listening to a struggling actor play the piano in a restaurant in the early 1960s?

RARTEWNBTEYA

ANSWER:

Arrange the circled letters to solve the mystery answer.

MYSTERY ANSWER

COUNTRY CAPITALS

JUMBLE BrainBusters!

Unscramble the Jumbles, one letter to each square, to spell country capitals.

#1 NIVEAN

#2 BUINLD

#3 VHAAAN

#4 WOSCOM

#5 AACRCSA

#6 SRUBSLSE

Box of Clues

Stumped? Maybe you can find a clue below.

-City on the Irish Sea
-Venezuela's capital
-Largest country's capital
-Belgium's capital
-Island country capital
-European city on the Atlantic
-Austria's capital

Arrange the circled letters to solve the mystery answer.

MYSTERY ANSWER

OCCUPATIONS

JUMBLE BrainBusters!

Unscramble the Jumbles, one letter to each square, to spell occupations.

#1 AOTIRL

#2 EUTBRL

#3 ROBERK

#4 ARSHEIC

#5 UORSGNE

#6 REEWJEL

Box of Clues

Stumped? Maybe you can find a clue below. (No clue for the Mystery Answer.)

-Starts with "B"; ends with "R"

-Starts with "S"; ends with "N"

-Starts with "T"; ends with "R"

-Starts with "B"; ends with "R"

-Starts with "J"; ends with "R"

-Starts with "C"; ends with "R"

Arrange the circled letters to solve the mystery answer.

MYSTERY ANSWER

WEATHER

Unscramble the Jumbles, one letter to each square, to spell words related to weather.

#1 AWMR

#2 AARRD

#3 MTROS

#4 LOEROC

#5 ZEEEBR

#6 NOARIWB

#7 NMOOONS

★ **JUMBLE® Trivia** Quick Quiz

Where would you have been if you had seen the first televised weather map in 1936?

NEGNDAL

ANSWER:

Arrange the circled letters to solve the mystery answer.

MYSTERY ANSWER

FOOTBALL

JUMBLE
BrainBusters!

Unscramble the Jumbles, one letter to each square, to spell words related to football.

#1 CTAHC

#2 OLKBC

#3 LACTEK

#4 LUMFEB

#5 KFKCFIO

#6 TENPLYA

★ JUMBLE® Trivia Quick Quiz

What would you be watching, if you were watching something that debuted during a televised football game in 1963?

TAISTANNRPLYE

ANSWER:

Arrange the circled letters to solve the mystery answer.

MYSTERY ANSWER

THE CIRCUS

Unscramble the Jumbles, one letter
to each square, to spell words related
to the circus.

#1 ETTN

#2 HSWO

#3 WLNOC

#4 RPTAEEZ

#5 BCOAATR

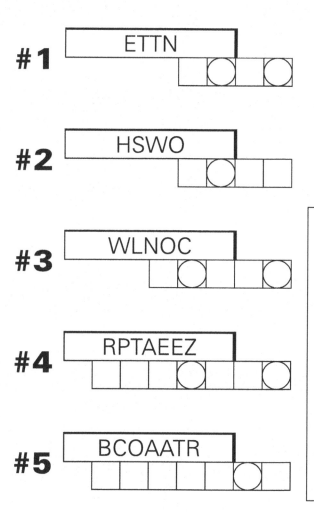

Interesting Circus Facts

The word "geek" originally referred to a circus sideshow person who bit the heads off chickens and snakes.

It takes about 200 people to assemble the 500 tons of equipment used in the Ringling Bros. and Barnum & Bailey Circus.

Arrange the circled letters
to solve the mystery answer.

MYSTERY ANSWER

ASIAN COUNTRIES

Unscramble the Jumbles, one letter to each square, to spell names of Asian countries.

#1 NIAID

#2 SIARY

#3 SRIUAS

#4 NVTMEIA

#5 SPAINKAT

#6 LONMAIOG

Strange Fact

The first letter of every continent's name is the same as the last letter.*

A̲fric̲a̲
A̲meric̲a̲
A̲ntarctic̲a̲
A̲si̲a̲
A̲ustrali̲a̲
E̲urop̲e̲

*Not counting "North" and "South."

Arrange the circled letters to solve the mystery answer.

MYSTERY ANSWER

CARNIVORES

Unscramble the Jumbles, one letter to each square, to spell carnivores.

#1 LNIO

#2 ETIRG

#3 NHAEY

#4 CAAJLK

#5 ADBERG

#6 LRIGZYZ

#7 RLOEADP

Carnivore

Carnivore is the term commonly applied to any animal whose diet consists wholly or largely of meat.

Over time, many carnivores have adapted to an omnivorous (mixed) diet.

Arrange the circled letters to solve the mystery answer.

MYSTERY ANSWER

TRANSPORTATION

JUMBLE BrainBusters!

Unscramble the Jumbles, one letter to each square, to spell words related to the transportation.

#1 NIRTA

#2 HAYTC

#3 RUKTC

#4 PBILM

#5 BUYSAW

#6 LICBCEY

Arrange the circled letters to solve the mystery answer.

Interesting Transportation Facts

Fiat stands for Fabbrica Italiana Automobile Torino.

The first subway was built in London in the mid-1800s.

The first person to die in an airplane accident was Lt. Thomas E. Selfridge, in 1908.

MYSTERY ANSWER

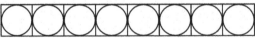

PLANET EARTH

Unscramble the Jumbles, one letter to each square, to spell words related to planet Earth.

#1 ACEV

#2 EAWRT

#3 NJLEUG

#4 LAVEYL

#5 RDTNAU

#6 GOLNOA

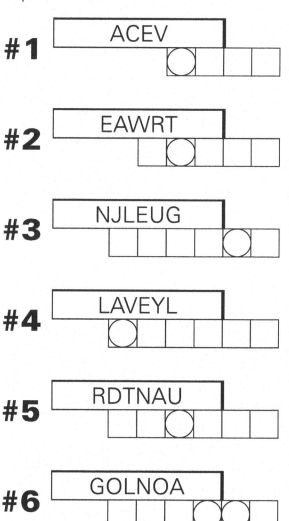

Interesting Planet Earth Facts

All living things on Earth contain carbon.

Each year, there are more than 50,000 earthquakes throughout the world.

Of all the water on Earth, only about 1.5 percent is fresh water.

Arrange the circled letters to solve the mystery answer.

MYSTERY ANSWER

MATH

JUMBLE BrainBusters!

Unscramble the Jumbled
letters, one letter to each square,
so that each equation is correct.

For example: NOLSOEPNEU
ONE PLUS ONE = TWO

#1 UTOWOOFRWT

◯☐☐ + ☐☐◯ = ☐◯☐☐

#2 SEOEGNENIHVTE

☐◯☐ + ☐☐☐◯☐ = ◯☐☐◯

#3 SFOFOUXIRTENREU

☐☐◯☐ × ☐☐◯☐ = ☐☐☐☐◯☐◯

#4 ROEFIOFEOVNEUN

☐☐◯ + ☐◯☐☐ = ☐☐◯☐ × ☐☐◯

#5 ZEIHTWTTGNEREOO

☐☐◯☐☐ + ◯☐☐ = ☐☐◯☐ + ☐◯☐☐

Then arrange the
circled letters to solve
the mystery equation.

MYSTERY EQUATION

◯◯◯ × ◯◯◯ = ◯◯◯◯◯◯ − ◯◯◯◯◯◯ + ◯◯◯

U.S. STATES

Unscramble the Jumbles, one letter
to each square, to spell names of
U.S. states.

#1 AHIWIA

#2 EAADNV

#3 OGERNO

#4 RLOFDIA

#5 NRIAOAZ

#6 TEKUNKYC

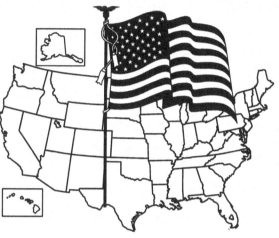

★ JUMBLE® Trivia Quick Quiz

What U.S. state would
you be in, if you were in
a U.S. state named after a
French king?

ALIOSIUAN

ANSWER:

Arrange the circled letters
to solve the mystery answer.

MYSTERY ANSWER

SCHOOL

JUMBLE
BrainBusters!

Unscramble the Jumbles, one letter to each square, to spell words related to school.

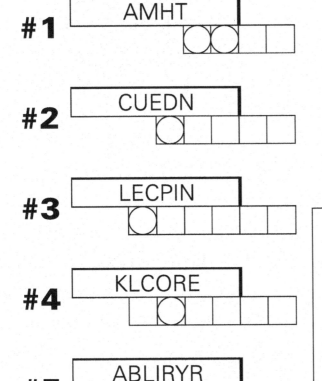

#1 AMHT

#2 CUEDN

#3 LECPIN

#4 KLCORE

#5 ABLIRYR

#6 GCLEEOL

Interesting School Facts

Research has shown that college graduates have longer life spans than people who do not complete high school.

More than 50 percent of teachers say they have bought books for their students with their own money, due to money and textbook shortages.

Arrange the circled letters to solve the mystery answer.

MYSTERY ANSWER

SITCOMS

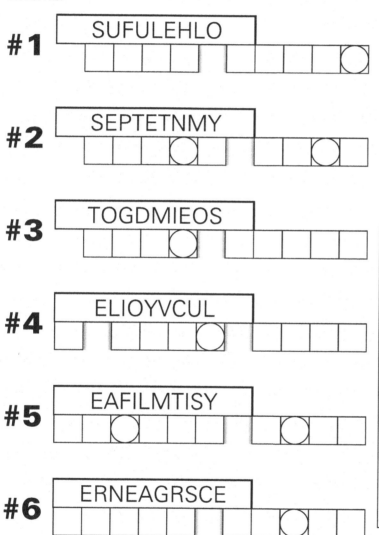

Unscramble the Jumbles, one letter to each square, to spell names of sitcoms.

#1 SUFULEHLO

#2 SEPTETNMY

#3 TOGDMIEOS

#4 ELIOYVCUL

#5 EAFILMTISY

#6 ERNEAGRSCE

Box of Clues

Stumped? Maybe you can find a clue below.

-E.A and E.G. sitcom 1965-1971
-Maude spin-off
-Top-rated show 1952-1955
-A.Y. and C.H. sitcom 1961-1965
-Popular NBC sitcom from 1982-1989
-R.M. sitcom 1988-1995
-Olsen twins sitcom 1987-1995

Arrange the circled letters to solve the mystery answer.

MYSTERY ANSWER

GEORGE WASHINGTON

Unscramble the Jumbles, one letter
to each square, to spell words related
to George Washington.

#1 HEFRNC

#2 RATMAH

#3 TVIRCOY

#4 NUCORYT

#5 GIRIVIAN

#6 REELDAAW

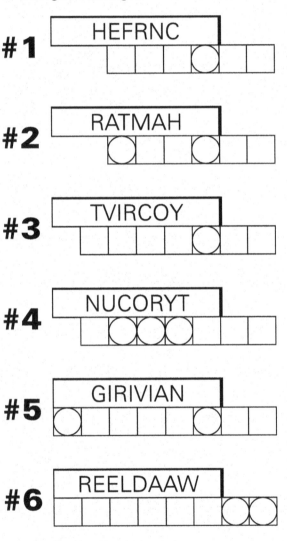

Box of Clues

Stumped? Maybe you can find a clue
below.

-Washington's enemy in 1754
-Washington's birth state
-Mrs. Washington
-River crossed in 1776
-Washington estate
-Washington's end result
 battling Cornwallis
-"The Father of His _____"

Arrange the circled letters
to solve the mystery answer.

MYSTERY ANSWER

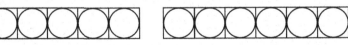

BIRDS

JUMBLE.
BrainBusters!

Unscramble the Jumbles, one letter
to each square, to spell types of birds.

#1 LUGL

#2 NIFHC

#3 OOGES

#4 ROSEYP

#5 RUTEYK

#6 CHNEICK

Interesting Bird Facts

There are more than 200 birds
that are classified as birds of
prey.

Certain birds of prey have
eyesight that is more than twice
as powerful as humans.

The Kori bustard (a type of bird)
can weigh up to 30 pounds.

Arrange the circled letters
to solve the mystery answer.

MYSTERY ANSWER

SOUTH AMERICA

JUMBLE BrainBusters!

Unscramble the Jumbles, one letter to each square, to spell words related to South America.

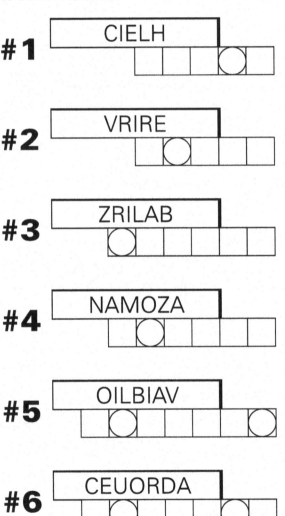

#1 CIELH

#2 VRIRE

#3 ZRILAB

#4 NAMOZA

#5 OILBIAV

#6 CEUORDA

Box of Clues

Stumped? Maybe you can find a clue below.

-Quito's home
-_____ rain forest
-Home to Bogota
-Largest South American country
-"Cold sounding" country
-Home to La Paz
-Amazon waterway

Arrange the circled letters to solve the mystery answer.

MYSTERY ANSWER

PLANTS

Unscramble the Jumbles, one letter to each square, to spell words related to plants.

#1 EAAGL

#2 OWSOD

#3 HCDOIR

#4 LPEONL

#5 CBARHN

#6 ELOFRW

Box of Clues

Stumped? Maybe you can find a clue below. (No clue for the Mystery Answer.)

-Bloom
-Stem subdivision
-Forest
-Flowering plant
-Kelp, for example
-Microspores

Arrange the circled letters to solve the mystery answer.

MYSTERY ANSWER

PRESIDENTS

Unscramble the Jumbles, one letter to each square, to spell last names of U.S. presidents.

#1 OPKL

#2 ARTGN

#3 LAYTRO

#4 EOHORV

#5 GRADNIH

#6 SJCKANO

Box of Clues

Stumped? Maybe you can find a clue clue. (No clue for the Mystery Answer.)

- Starts with "H"; ends with "R"
- Starts with "J"; ends with "N"
- Starts with "P"; ends with "K"
- Starts with "H"; ends with "G"
- Starts with "G"; ends with "T"
- Starts with "T"; ends with "R"

Arrange the circled letters to solve the mystery answer.

MYSTERY ANSWER

COUNTRIES

Unscramble the Jumbles, one letter to each square, to spell names of countries.

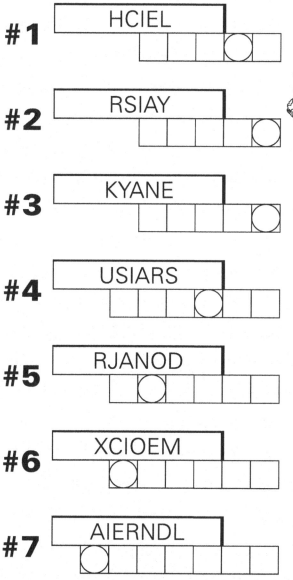

#1 HCIEL

#2 RSIAY

#3 KYANE

#4 USIARS

#5 RJANOD

#6 XCIOEM

#7 AIERNDL

Mystery Answer Facts

-Home to about 8 million
-Takes up about 250,000 square miles
-Lies south of the Arabian Peninsula
-Borders the Indian Ocean
-Home to Mogadishu

Arrange the circled letters to solve the mystery answer.

MYSTERY ANSWER

WEATHER

Unscramble the Jumbles, one letter to each square, to spell words related to weather.

#1 EKLAF

#2 OGYGF

#3 NIYDW

#4 LHICYL

#5 EEEGRD

#6 UDHTERN

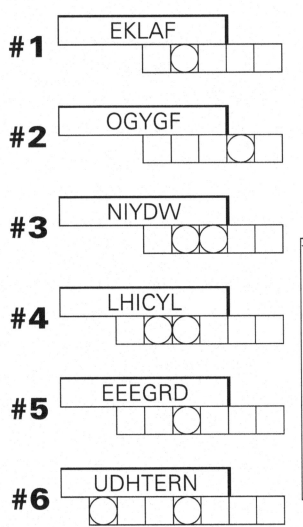

Arrange the circled letters to solve the mystery answer.

★ **JUMBLE® Trivia** Quick Quiz

Where might you have been in 1928, if you were on an island when a hurricane dumped 30 inches of rain?

TUECRORPIO

ANSWER:

MYSTERY ANSWER

MUSICAL INSTRUMENTS

Unscramble the Jumbles, one letter to each square, to spell names of musical instruments.

#1 OEOB

#2 RDMU

#3 LUETF

#4 NIOILV

#5 NEORTC

#6 SAOBNOS

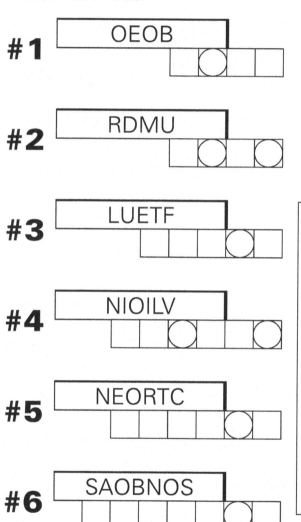

Interesting Music Facts

The working section of a piano is called the action.

When he was 14, Wynton Marsalis played the trumpet with the New Orleans Philharmonic.

The word piano is short for the instrument's original name, piano et forte, which means soft and loud.

Arrange the circled letters to solve the mystery answer.

MYSTERY ANSWER

PLANET EARTH

Unscramble the Jumbles, one letter to each square, to spell words related to planet Earth.

#1 FLFUB

#2 YSBSA

#3 LBOGE

#4 SEEGRY

#5 GAOLNO

#6 CURSFEA

Box of Clues

Stumped? Maybe you can find a clue below.

- Shallow body of water
- Deep gulf
- Earth model
- Type of science
- Powerful spring
- Crust's top
- Steep bank

Arrange the circled letters to solve the mystery answer.

MYSTERY ANSWER

EUROPEAN COUNTRIES

Unscramble the Jumbles, one letter
to each square, to spell names of
European countries.

#1 AONDLP

#2 RONWYA

#3 AFILNDN

#4 AEDGLNN

#5 RUHNAYG

#6 AGREYNM

Interesting
Facts About Europe

France and Italy produce over
40% of the world's wine.

Coffee was first imported into
Europe in the early 1500s.

The only true desert in Europe
is the Bledowska Desert in
Poland.

Arrange the circled letters
to solve the mystery answer.

MYSTERY ANSWER

CALIFORNIA

Unscramble the Jumbles, one letter to each square, to spell words related to California.

#1 EIWN

#2 AOTEH

#3 LAEVYL

#4 NRFEOS

#5 AACECSDS

#6 TOSYEIEM

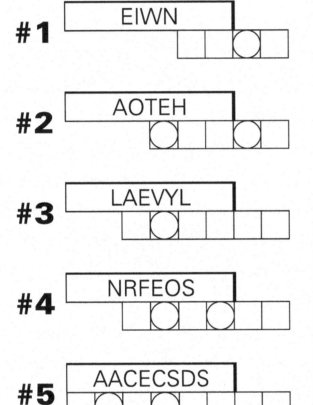

Box of Clues

Stumped? Maybe you can find a clue below.

- Lake _____
- Northern California mountains
- Capital
- National park
- Death _____
- Central California city
- Napa Valley export

Arrange the circled letters to solve the mystery answer.

MYSTERY ANSWER

SCIENCE

Unscramble the Jumbles, one letter to each square, to spell words related to science.

#1 EGYERN

#2 TEARTM

#3 WEONNT

#4 YNAAEZL

#5 NLEETME

#6 OOMCUPDN

Box of Clues

Stumped? Maybe you can find a clue below.

- Study
- Substance of which a physical object is composed
- Branch of knowledge that deals with the structure of organisms
- Power
- Helium or gold
- H_2O, for example
- English mathematician, physicist

MYSTERY ANSWER

Arrange the circled letters to solve the mystery answer.

SPORTS

Unscramble the Jumbles, one letter to each square, to spell words related to sports.

#1 GITFH

#2 ROERR

#3 MEHRO

#4 GNININ

#5 CHOYEK

#6 GOUDUT

Box of Clues

Stumped? Maybe you can find a clue below. (No clue for the Mystery Answer.)

-Mistake
-Slick sport
-Bout
-Waiting area
-Reason to trot
-Baseball increment

Arrange the circled letters to solve the mystery answer.

MYSTERY ANSWER

U.S. STATE CAPITALS

JUMBLE BrainBusters!

Unscramble the Jumbles, one letter to each square, to spell names of U.S. state capitals.

#1 BAALYN

#2 NUEJUA

#3 POKTAE

#4 NLNICLO

#5 ASNNLIG

#6 PNHOIXE

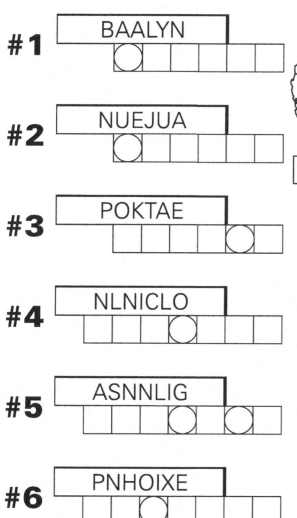

★ JUMBLE® Trivia Quick Quiz

Where would you be standing, if you were standing in the U.S. state capital at 30n latitude and 84w longitude?

EALAATSSELH

ANSWER:

Arrange the circled letters to solve the mystery answer.

MYSTERY ANSWER

ACTORS & ACTRESSES

JUMBLE BrainBusters!

Unscramble the Jumbles, one letter to each square, to spell the names of actors and actresses.

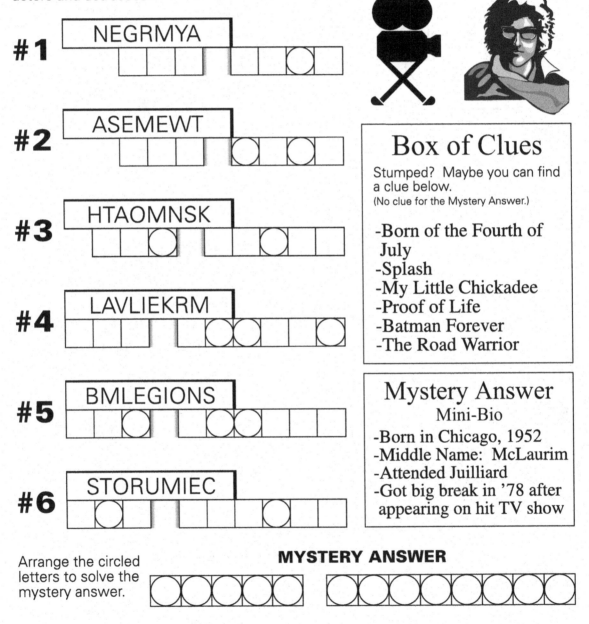

#1 NEGRMYA

#2 ASEMEWT

#3 HTAOMNSK

#4 LAVLIEKRM

#5 BMLEGIONS

#6 STORUMIEC

Box of Clues

Stumped? Maybe you can find a clue below.
(No clue for the Mystery Answer.)

-Born of the Fourth of July
-Splash
-My Little Chickadee
-Proof of Life
-Batman Forever
-The Road Warrior

Mystery Answer
Mini-Bio

-Born in Chicago, 1952
-Middle Name: McLaurim
-Attended Juilliard
-Got big break in '78 after appearing on hit TV show

Arrange the circled letters to solve the mystery answer.

MYSTERY ANSWER

FOOD

JUMBLE BrainBusters!

Unscramble the Jumbles, one letter to each square, to spell words related to food.

#1 NODTU

#2 OIECKO

#3 RPPPEE

#4 TEUBRT

#5 ERCLEA

#6 UFIFNM

Box of Clues

Stumped? Maybe you can find a clue below. (No clue for the Mystery Answer.)

-Starts with "B"; ends with "R"

-Starts with "P"; ends with "R"

-Starts with "C"; ends with "E"

-Starts with "C"; ends with "L"

-Starts with "M"; ends with "N"

-Starts with "D"; ends with "T"

Arrange the circled letters to solve the mystery answer.

MYSTERY ANSWER

NORTH AMERICA

JUMBLE.
BrainBusters!

Unscramble the Jumbles, one letter to each square, to spell words related to North America.

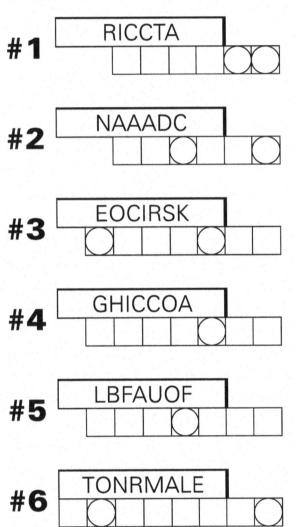

#1 RICCTA

#2 NAAADC

#3 EOCIRSK

#4 GHICCOA

#5 LBFAUOF

#6 TONRMALE

Arrange the circled letters to solve the mystery answer.

Box of Clues

Stumped? Maybe you can find a clue below.

-U.S. city or North American mammal
-Extreme northern region
-Large Canadian city
-Continental Divide divider
-Lake Michigan city
-The most populous of its kind in the U.S.
-Hudson Bay's home

MYSTERY ANSWER

MOVIES

Unscramble the Jumbles, one letter to each square, to spell spell titles of movies.

#1 UCAB

#2 RFAOG

#3 FHEIMTR

#4 TANFSIAA

#5 ZOGDLLIA

#6 LGAMNIAO

Box of Clues

Stumped? Maybe you can find a clue below.

-1993 Tom Cruise movie
-1996 Coen brothers movie
-1979 Sean Connery movie
-1999 Jason Robards movie
-1940 Disney movie
-1996 Billy Bob Thornton movie
-1998 Matthew Broderick monster movie

Arrange the circled letters to solve the mystery answer.

MYSTERY ANSWER

U.S. CITIES

Unscramble the Jumbles, one letter to each square, to spell names of U.S. cities.

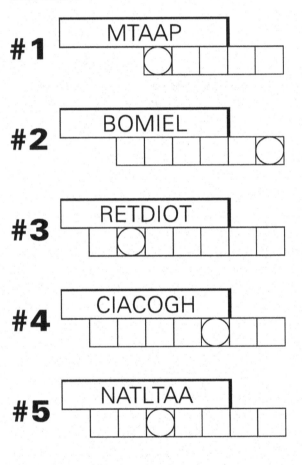

#1 MTAAP

#2 BOMIEL

#3 RETDIOT

#4 CIACOGH

#5 NATLTAA

#6 SOUHONT

Box of Clues

Stumped? Maybe you can find a clue below. (No clue for the Mystery Answer.)

-Alabama city
-"The Motor City"
-City on Lake Michigan
-Largest Texas city
-Florida bay city
-Georgia city

Arrange the circled letters to solve the mystery answer.

MYSTERY ANSWER

TV SHOWS

JUMBLE BrainBusters!

Unscramble the Jumbles, one letter to each square, to spell names of TV shows.

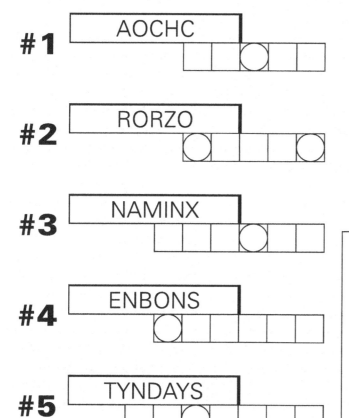

#1 AOCHC

#2 RORZO

#3 NAMINX

#4 ENBONS

#5 TYNDAYS

#6 NSOERANE

Box of Clues

Stumped? Maybe you can find a clue below.

-ABC, 1979-1986, sitcom
-ABC, 1957-1859, Western
-NBC, 1959-1973, Western
-ABC, 1989-1997, sitcom
-ABC, 1981-1989, drama
-ABC, 1988-1997, sitcom
-CBS, 1967-1975, detective drama

Arrange the circled letters to solve the mystery answer.

MYSTERY ANSWER

POETRY

JUMBLE BrainBusters!

Unscramble the Jumbles, one letter to each square, to spell words found in the poem.

#1 TEADEB

#2 VEANSEL

#3 GTIHM

#4 HFTIG

#5 BMFELU

#6 MLJUEB

WORDS by Kim Nolan

Words can _____ #1
And words can agree
Some words _____ #2
While others set free

Some words are meek
Yet others have _____ #3
Some words resolve
While other words _____ #4

Some words have grace
While some words _____ #5
Some words stand straight
And some words _____ #6

Arrange the circled letters
to solve the mystery answer.
(The mystery answer is not
in the poem.)

MYSTERY ANSWER

THE HUMAN BODY

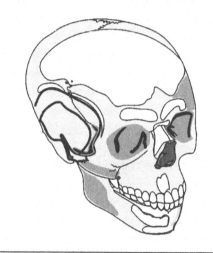

Unscramble the Jumbles, one letter to each square, to spell words related to the human body.

#1 NLGDA

#2 BIFUAL

#3 EDIYNK

#4 XTOARH

#5 LSUECM

#6 ANEMLE

Arrange the circled letters to solve the mystery answer.

★ JUMBLE® Trivia Quick Quiz

What would you be using, if you were using the area of the brain that allows humans to hear and understand speech?

LRMPTABOELOE

ANSWER:

MYSTERY ANSWER

SPORTS

Unscramble the Jumbles, one letter to each square, to spell words related to sports.

#1 GUBRY

#2 OCBKL

#3 TCAHC

#4 ESBTKA

#5 LBMUEF

#6 BRIDEBL

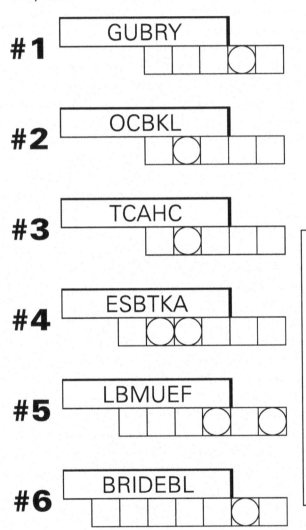

Interesting Sports Facts

The official flag of the Olympic Games was introduced in 1920.

Monday Night Football debuted in 1970.

More than half of professional hockey players have lost at least one tooth while playing.

Arrange the circled letters to solve the mystery answer.

MYSTERY ANSWER

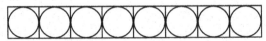

OUTER SPACE

JUMBLE BrainBusters!

Unscramble the Jumbles, one letter to each square, to spell words related to outer space.

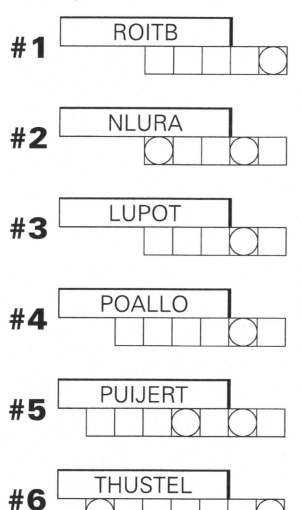

#1 ROITB

#2 NLURA

#3 LUPOT

#4 POALLO

#5 PUIJERT

#6 THUSTEL

Box of Clues

Stumped? Maybe you can find a clue below. (No clue for the Mystery Answer.)

- Relating to the moon
- Moon landing mission
- NASA spaceship
- Circular motion
- Gigantic planet
- Small planet

Arrange the circled letters to solve the mystery answer.

MYSTERY ANSWER

TV SHOWS

Unscramble the Jumbles, one letter
to each square, to spell names of
TV shows.

#1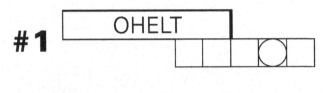
OHELT

#2
ACNNNO

#3
CMTOAKL

#4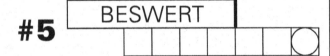
WNEARTH

#5
BESWERT

#6
LAURONTG

Box of Clues

Stumped? Maybe you can find a
clue below.

-CBS drama starring E.A.
(1977-1982)
-NBC police drama starring
F.D. (1984-1991)
-CBS detective drama starring
W.C. (1971-1976)
-ABC drama starring J.B. and
C.S. (1983-1988)
-ABC sitcom starring E.L.
(1983-1987)
-CBS sitcom starring B.N.
(1982-1990)
-NBC / ABC legal drama
starring A.G. (1986-1995)

Arrange the circled letters
to solve the mystery answer.

MYSTERY ANSWER

ALL ABOUT ALASKA

JUMBLE BrainBusters!

Unscramble the Jumbles, one letter to each square, to spell words related to Alaska.

#1 DOKIKA

#2 RUTNAD

#3 LAEZDV

#4 AUNJUE

#5 ALIGERC

#6 ECKMILYN

Box of Clues

Stumped? Maybe you can find a clue below. (No clue for the Mystery Answer.)

-Capital
-Icy formation
-Alaskan island and city
-Alaskan mountain
-City on Prince William Sound
-Treeless plain

Arrange the circled letters to solve the mystery answer.

MYSTERY ANSWER

MOVIES

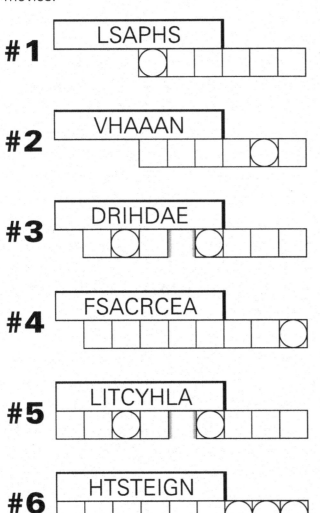

**JUMBLE.
BrainBusters!**

Unscramble the Jumbles, one letter to each square, to spell titles of movies.

#1 LSAPHS

#2 VHAAAN

#3 DRIHDAE

#4 FSACRCEA

#5 LITCYHLA

#6 HTSTEIGN

Box of Clues

Stumped? Maybe you can find a clue below.

- 1996 Al Pacino movie set in NYC
- 1980 Jack Nicholson movie
- 1990 movie set in Cuba
- 1988 Bruce Willis movie
- 1973 Redford, Newman movie
- 1984 Tom Hanks movie
- 1983 Al Pacino movie

Arrange the circled letters to solve the mystery answer.

MYSTERY ANSWER

AMERICAN INDIANS

Unscramble the Jumbles, one letter to each square, to spell names of American Indian tribes.

#1 VAJOAN

#2 HPAECA

#3 HAAORAP

#4 AOHMINC

#5 EHASNEW

#6 CREHEKOE

Box of Clues

Stumped? Maybe you can find a clue below.

- Starts with "A"; ends with "E"
- Starts with "S"; ends with "E"
- Starts with "C"; ends with "W"
- Starts with "A"; ends with "O"
- Starts with "M"; ends with "N"
- Starts with "N"; ends with "O"
- Starts with "C"; ends with "E"

Arrange the circled letters to solve the mystery answer.

MYSTERY ANSWER

AUSTRALIA

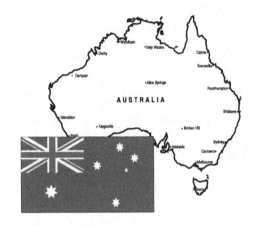

JUMBLE. BrainBusters!

Unscramble the Jumbles, one letter to each square, to spell words related to Australia.

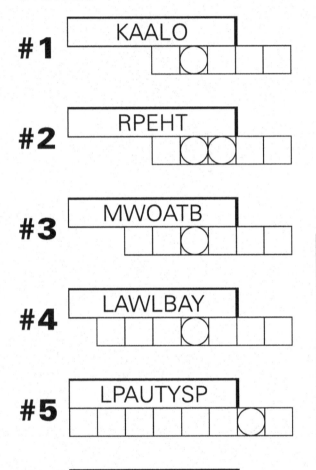

#1 KAALO

#2 RPEHT

#3 MWOATB

#4 LAWLBAY

#5 LPAUTYSP

#6 ACNBREAR

Box of Clues

Stumped? Maybe you can find a clue below.

- Billed mammal
- Capital city
- Stocky marsupial
- Second largest city
- Small kangaroo
- Largest west coast city
- Marsupial with hairy ears

Arrange the circled letters to solve the mystery answer.

MYSTERY ANSWER

ACTORS & ACTRESSES

JUMBLE. BrainBusters!

Unscramble the Jumbles, one letter to each square, to spell the names of actors and actresses.

#1 BEGMILONS

#2 RESNERSUO

#3 VAIMYIRNG

#4 SJMEACANA

#5 HJOCCUNSKA

#6 BATKHYAEST

Box of Clues

Stumped? Maybe you can find a clue below.

- Eraser, Mickey Blue Eyes
- Get Shorty, Tin Cup
- Deconstructing Harry, Micki & Maude
- Better Off Dead, High Fidelity
- What Women Want, Payback
- Misery, Primary Colors
- Stepmom, I Love Trouble

Arrange the circled letters to solve the mystery answer.

MYSTERY ANSWER

ANIMALS

JUMBLE
BrainBusters!

Unscramble the Jumbles, one letter to each square, to spell names of animals.

#1 RIETG

#2 AJALKC

#3 OBONAB

#4 PINEUNG

#5 ACEHETH

#6 KSMRTAU

★ JUMBLE® Trivia Quick Quiz

What would you be holding if you were holding an animal that had a tongue that was more than 1.5 times the length of its body?

MLAEHONEC

ANSWER:

Arrange the circled letters to solve the mystery answer.

MYSTERY ANSWER

AROUND THE HOME

JUMBLE BrainBusters!

Unscramble the Jumbles, one letter to each square, to spell words related to the home.

#1 ATELB

#2 RAFEM

#3 TUOETL

#4 RPNATY

#5 RGGAEA

#6 NWDWIO

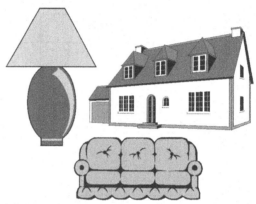

Box of Clues

Stumped? Maybe you can find a clue below. (No clue for the Mystery Answer.)

-Starts with "W"; ends with "W"

-Starts with "F"; ends with "E"

-Starts with "O"; ends with "T"

-Starts with "T"; ends with "E"

-Starts with "G"; ends with "E"

-Starts with "P"; ends with "Y"

Arrange the circled letters to solve the mystery answer.

MYSTERY ANSWER

BIRDS

Unscramble the Jumbles, one letter to each square, to spell types of birds.

#1 OLNO

#2 CIFHN

#3 ARVNE

#4 AMAWC

#5 UPENING

#6 LVURTEU

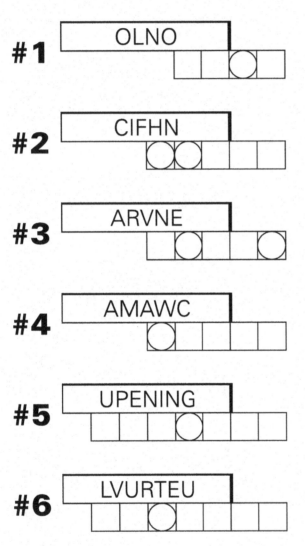

Box of Clues

Stumped? Maybe you can find a clue below.

-Starts with "P"; ends with "N"

-Starts with "M"; ends with "W"

-Starts with "L"; ends with "N"

-Starts with "F"; ends with "O"

-Starts with "R"; ends with "N"

-Starts with "F"; ends with "H"

-Starts with "V"; ends with "E"

Arrange the circled letters to solve the mystery answer.

MYSTERY ANSWER

CLOTHING & FASHION

Unscramble the Jumbles, one letter to each square, to spell words related to clothing and fashion.

#1 YONNL

#2 SRESD

#3 AEJSN

#4 AAELPRP

#5 TESWARE

#6 ARGENTM

Box of Clues

Stumped? Maybe you can find a clue below. (No clue for the Mystery Answer.)

-Cool weather garment
-Clothing
-Style of pants
-Hosiery material
-Article of clothing
-Woman's garment

Arrange the circled letters to solve the mystery answer.

MYSTERY ANSWER

AUTOMOBILES

Unscramble the Jumbles, one letter to each square, to spell words related to automobiles.

#1 CRKUT

#2 RUKNT

#3 EWIRP

#4 CPIUPK

#5 PBMRUE

#6 HEAUXTS

Interesting Automobile Facts

Private cars were not allowed on Bermuda until 1948. Most people got around on bicycles.

More Americans have died in auto accidents than have died in all wars fought by the United States.

Arrange the circled letters to solve the mystery answer.

MYSTERY ANSWER

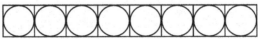

JUMBLE®

BrainBusters!

ADVANCED PUZZLES

ALL ABOUT MUSIC

JUMBLE BrainBusters!

Unscramble the Jumbles, one letter to each square, to spell words related to music.

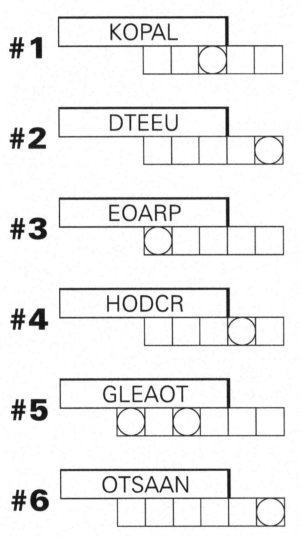

#1 KOPAL

#2 DTEEU

#3 EOARP

#4 HODCR

#5 GLEAOT

#6 OTSAAN

Box of Clues

Stumped? Maybe you can find a clue below. (No clue for the Mystery Answer.)

-Three or more tones played together
-Musical drama
-Lively dance music
-Smooth musical style
-Instrumental composition
-Practice piece

Arrange the circled letters to solve the mystery answer.

MYSTERY ANSWER

WEATHER

Unscramble the Jumbles, one letter to each square, to spell words related to weather.

#1 AILH

#2 CICLIE

#3 OSARIB

#4 GEEERD

#5 ULCYDO

#6 MNUISB

Box of Clues

Stumped? Maybe you can find a clue below.

-Frozen formation
-Powerful storm
-Temperature unit
-Line of equal pressure
-Frozen precipitation
-Cloud type
-Overcast

Arrange the circled letters to solve the mystery answer.

MYSTERY ANSWER

ALL ABOUT DOGS

JUMBLE. BrainBusters!

Unscramble the Jumbles, one letter to each square, to spell types of dogs.

#1 RBXEO

#2 DHNUO

#3 SHYUK

#4 AGBLEE

#5 ASIPELN

#6 LOULBDG

#7 BORADNME

Interesting Dog Facts

The average life span of a dog is about 11 years. The cost of owning a dog for the whole 11 years is approximately $13,000.

Some of the oldest dog breeds are thought to have been developed about 3,000 B.C.

Arrange the circled letters to solve the mystery answer.

MYSTERY ANSWER

PRESIDENTS' FIRST NAMES

Unscramble the Jumbles, one letter to each square, to spell first names of U.S. presidents.

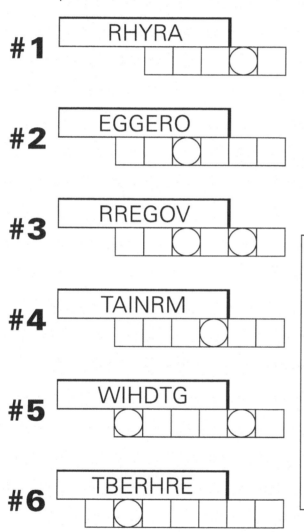

#1 RHYRA

#2 EGGERO

#3 RREGOV

#4 TAINRM

#5 WIHDTG

#6 TBERHRE

Interesting Presidential Facts

Arnold Schwarzenegger bought President John F. Kennedy's golf clubs at an auction in 1996. He paid $772,500.

The first woman to run for president of the United States was Victoria Woodhall. She ran in 1872.

Arrange the circled letters to solve the mystery answer.

MYSTERY ANSWER

MATH

**JUMBLE.
BrainBusters!**

Unscramble the Jumbled
letters, one letter to each square,
so that each equation is correct.

For example: NOLSOEPNEU
ONE PLUS ONE = TWO

#1 WTOOZEWROT

☐☐◯ – ◯☐☐ = ◯☐☐☐

#2 HNEOURTEFEOR

◯☐☐ + ☐◯☐◯☐ = ◯☐☐☐

#3 FISETOVEVNWE

☐☐☐◯ + ☐☐◯ = ☐☐◯☐

#4 NOONNIEEENNIEN

☐◯☐ + ☐☐◯☐ – ☐☐◯☐ = ☐◯☐◯

#5 EOHTNFURRETEEHETR

☐◯☐ – ☐☐☐◯☐ = ☐☐☐◯☐ + ☐☐◯☐☐

Then arrange the
circled letters to solve
the mystery equation. **MYSTERY EQUATION**

◯◯◯ + ◯◯◯◯ – ◯◯◯◯◯ = ◯◯◯◯◯ – ◯◯◯◯◯◯

COUNTRIES

JUMBLE
BrainBusters!

Unscramble the Jumbles, one letter to each square, to spell names of countries.

#1 ARILBZ

#2 EERGCE

#3 WESEND

#4 TUSAIAR

#5 MAAJCIA

#6 GBMLUIE

★ JUMBLE® Trivia Quick Quiz

Where would you be, if you were in the country that is the world's number one producer of cork?

APROGLUT

ANSWER:

Arrange the circled letters to solve the mystery answer.

MYSTERY ANSWER

ISLANDS

Unscramble the Jumbles, one letter to each square, to spell names of islands.

#1 BRAUA

#2 LMAAT

#3 SCIYIL

#4 WAINTA

#5 TNIUAAG

#6 DERBMAU

Box of Clues

Stumped? Maybe you can find a clue below. (No clue for the Mystery Answer.)

-Starts with "S", Ends with "Y"
-Starts with "A", Ends with "A"
-Starts with "A", Ends with "A"
-Starts with "M", Ends with "A"
-Starts with "B", Ends with "A"
-Starts with "T", Ends with "N"

Arrange the circled letters to solve the mystery answer.

MYSTERY ANSWER

GARDENING

Unscramble the Jumbles, one letter to each square, to spell words related to gardening.

#1 TLAPN

#2 URPEN

#3 USHUM

#4 VHOSLE

#5 OLERFW

#6 SCOPTOM

Interesting Gardening Fact

Cape Town, South Africa is home to Kirstenbosch Botanical Gardens. There are more than 6,000 species of plants grown there.

Tomato vines can be toxic if eaten.

Arrange the circled letters to solve the mystery answer.

MYSTERY ANSWER

CLASSIC ACTORS

JUMBLE BrainBusters!

Unscramble the Jumbles, one letter to each square, to spell last names of classic actors.

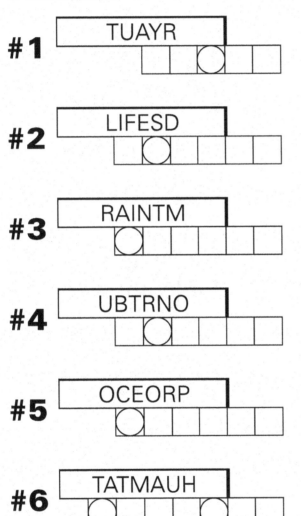

#1 TUAYR

#2 LIFESD

#3 RAINTM

#4 UBTRNO

#5 OCEORP

#6 TATMAUH

Box of Clues

Stumped? Maybe you can find a clue below.

-W.C. _____
-Dean _____
-Robert _____
-Richard _____
-Jackie _____
-Gene _____
-Walter _____

Arrange the circled letters to solve the mystery answer.

MYSTERY ANSWER

ALL ABOUT PLANTS

Unscramble the Jumbles, one letter to each square, to spell words related to plants.

#1 ERTE

#2 GITLH

#3 KTNRU

#4 EARWT

#5 NBTOYA

#6 TCCSUA

Interesting Plant Facts

There are hundreds of thousands of flowering plants on Earth.

The leaves of some plants will assume a different position at night, as a result of the lack of light. This process is called nyctitropism.

Arrange the circled letters to solve the mystery answer.

MYSTERY ANSWER

SOUTH AMERICA

JUMBLE
BrainBusters!

Unscramble the Jumbles, one letter to each square, to spell words related to the South America.

#1 RZIBLA

#2 VBIOLIA

#3 CIPAICF

#4 GURAUYU

#5 RCAAASC

#6 NALATICT

Box of Clues

Stumped? Maybe you can find a clue below.

- Home to Rio de Janeiro
- Home to Montevideo
- Venezuela's capital
- Western border
- Home to La Paz
- Eastern border
- The capital of Chile

Arrange the circled letters to solve the mystery answer.

MYSTERY ANSWER

TV SHOWS

Unscramble the Jumbles, one letter to each square, to spell names of TV shows.

#1 OSPA

#2 JKOKA

#3 MAFIYL

#4 FNUKUG

#5 TYDANYS

#6 TARBETA

Box of Clues

Stumped? Maybe you can find a clue below.

- Carradine show
- Kristy McNichol show
- T.S.'s detective show
- Long-running TV Western
- Controversial ABC sitcom
- Robert Blake's show 1975-1978
- Nighttime soap

Arrange the circled letters to solve the mystery answer.

MYSTERY ANSWER

U.S. STATE CAPITALS

Unscramble the Jumbles, one letter
to each square, to spell names of U.S.
state capitals.

#1 RIEEPR

#2 PTOKAE

#3 SOOBNT

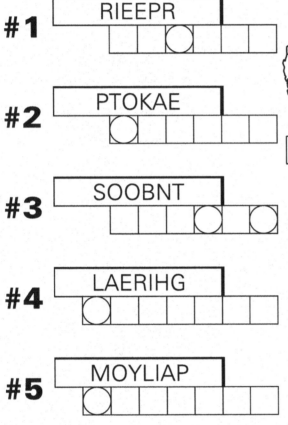

#4 LAERIHG

#5 MOYLIAP

#6 LAATNAT

Interesting State Capital Facts

The northernmost U.S. state capital is Juneau, Alaska.

The southernmost U.S. state capital is Honolulu, Hawaii.

Pennsylvania's capital, Harrisburg, was named after the city's founder, John Harris.

Arrange the circled letters
to solve the mystery answer.

MYSTERY ANSWER

SPORTS

JUMBLE BrainBusters!

Unscramble the Jumbles, one letter to each square, to spell words related to sports.

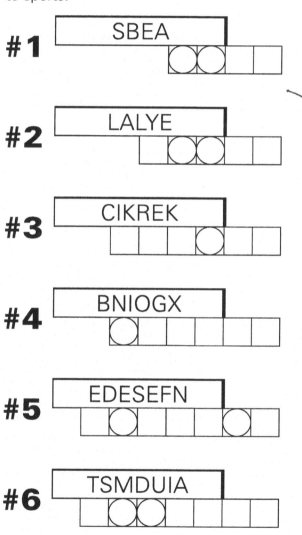

#1 SBEA

#2 LALYE

#3 CIKREK

#4 BNIOGX

#5 EDESEFN

#6 TSMDUIA

Box of Clues

Stumped? Maybe you can find a clue below. (No clue for the Mystery Answer.)

-Football position
-Lane
-"Round" sport
-Offense's opponent
-Playing area
-Diamond corner

Arrange the circled letters to solve the mystery answer.

MYSTERY ANSWER

MOVIES

JUMBLE BrainBusters!

Unscramble the Jumbles, one letter to each square, to spell titles of movies.

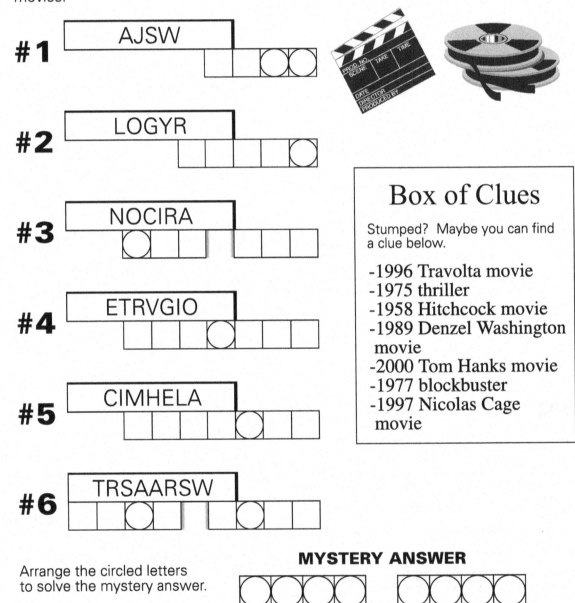

#1 AJSW

#2 LOGYR

#3 NOCIRA

#4 ETRVGIO

#5 CIMHELA

#6 TRSAARSW

Box of Clues

Stumped? Maybe you can find a clue below.

- -1996 Travolta movie
- -1975 thriller
- -1958 Hitchcock movie
- -1989 Denzel Washington movie
- -2000 Tom Hanks movie
- -1977 blockbuster
- -1997 Nicolas Cage movie

Arrange the circled letters to solve the mystery answer.

MYSTERY ANSWER

U.S. CITIES

Unscramble the Jumbles, one letter to each square, to spell names of U.S. cities.

#1 ADALSL

#2 TDEIOTR

#3 CIOCAHG

#4 LATAANT

#5 LOKAADN

#6 FBAUOLF

Arrange the circled letters to solve the mystery answer.

Box of Clues

Stumped? Maybe you can find a clue below. (No clue for the Mystery Answer.)

- Home to Joe Louis Arena
- Niagara River city
- Bay area city
- Home to Carter Presidential Center
- Trinity River city
- Home to Soldier Field

MYSTERY ANSWER

ALL ABOUT MONEY

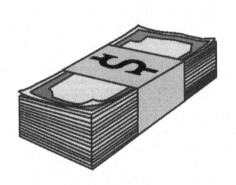

Unscramble the Jumbles, one letter
to each square, to spell words related
to money.

#1 ABKN

#2 BDITE

#3 GHCAER

#4 PECRITE

#5 TCAONUC

#6 APEMTNY

Box of Clues

Stumped? Maybe you can find a clue
below. (No clue for the Mystery Answer.)

-Pay later
-Lending institution
-Checking _____
-Charge against a bank account
-Proof of purchase
-Down _____

Arrange the circled letters
to solve the mystery answer.

MYSTERY ANSWER

ANIMALS

Unscramble the Jumbles, one letter to each square, to spell names of animals.

#1 AHNEY

#2 EGSOO

#3 ELRUM

#4 SOMOE

#5 NGIOPE

#6 HOGREP

#7 LORGIAL

Mystery Answer Facts

-Type of rodent
-Likes to nest underground
-Eats grasses, roots and insects
-Classified in the phylum Chordata
-Likes to swarm with others of its kind

Arrange the circled letters to solve the mystery answer.

MYSTERY ANSWER

FAMOUS ATHLETES

Unscramble the Jumbles, one letter to each square, to spell names of famous athletes.

#1 BDIR

#2 UASNIT

#3 SAGSIA

#4 EIHGRG

#5 UTUSKB

#6 LEONNS

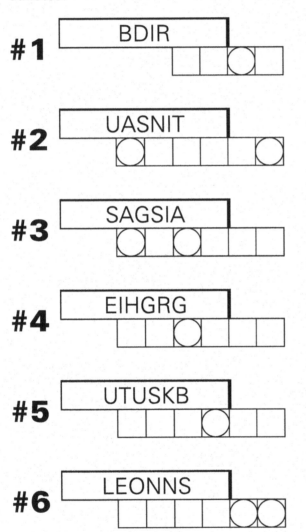

Box of Clues

Stumped? Maybe you can find a clue below.

-Yankee Lou
-Flying Celtic
-Swinging Byron
-Tennis player Tracy
-Famous slugger
-Football Dick
-Andre _____

Arrange the circled letters to solve the mystery answer.

MYSTERY ANSWER

U.S. STATES

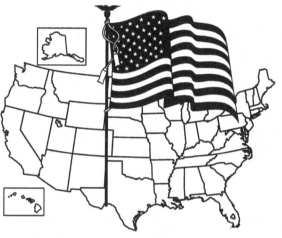

Unscramble the Jumbles, one letter to each square, to spell names of U.S. states.

#1 EIMAN

#2 KLAASA

#3 ROEONG

#4 EGGOIAR

#5 TANNAOM

#6 ESNBAKAR

Box of Clues

Stumped? Maybe you can find a clue below.

-4th state to enter Union (1788)
-33rd state to enter Union (1859)
-49th state to enter Union (1959)
-16th state to enter Union (1796)
-23rd state to enter Union (1820)
-37th state to enter Union (1867)
-41st state to enter Union (1889)

Arrange the circled letters to solve the mystery answer.

MYSTERY ANSWER

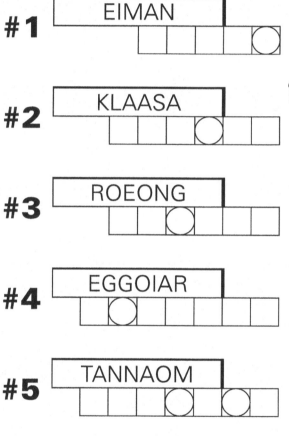

PRESIDENTS

Unscramble the Jumbles, one letter to each square, to spell last names of U.S. presidents.

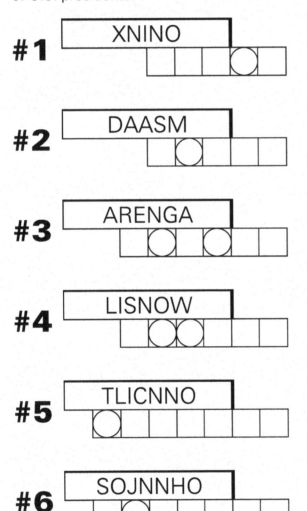

#1 XNINO

#2 DAASM

#3 ARENGA

#4 LISNOW

#5 TLICNNO

#6 SOJNNHO

Box of Clues

Stumped? Maybe you can find a clue below. (No clue for the Mystery Answer.)

-Rhodes scholar
-First president to resign
-17th or 36th
-Princeton graduate (1879)
-Nancy's husband
-Second or Sixth

Arrange the circled letters to solve the mystery answer.

MYSTERY ANSWER

SCHOOL

Unscramble the Jumbles, one letter to each square, to spell words related to school.

#1 MHTA

#2 ERNAL

#3 UFLNK

#4 OUIJRN

#5 SMOTAC

#6 TISHOYR

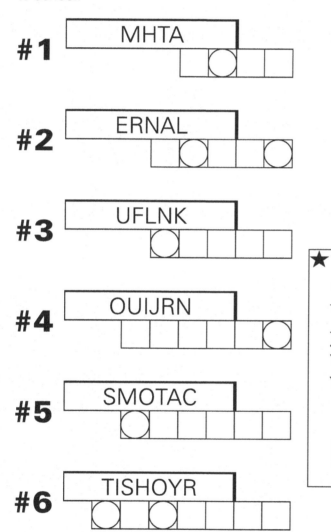

★ JUMBLE® Trivia Quick Quiz

What college town would you be standing in, if you were standing in a town with a 08544 zip code?

TRIPCENNO

ANSWER:

Arrange the circled letters to solve the mystery answer.

MYSTERY ANSWER

SITCOMS

Unscramble the Jumbles, one letter to each square, to spell names of sitcoms.

#1 UAEMD

#2 UNSSER

#3 KIORWGN

#4 HENATRW

#5 OMLSBOS

#6 DENISFLE

Arrange the circled letters to solve the mystery answer.

Box of Clues

Stumped? Maybe you can find a clue below.

- NBC sitcom (debuted in 1993)
- CBS sitcom (debuted in 1972)
- NBC sitcom (debuted in 1997)
- NBC sitcom (debuted in 1991)
- CBS sitcom (debuted in 1982)
- NBC sitcom (debuted in 1991)
- NBC sitcom (debuted in 1990)

MYSTERY ANSWER

FOOD

JUMBLE BrainBusters!

Unscramble the Jumbles, one letter to each square, to spell words related to food.

#1 HSUIS

#2 LERIHS

#3 NAIDHS

#4 RCEALE

#5 SBIUCIT

#6 ROPCPNO

Box of Clues

Stumped? Maybe you can find a clue below.

- Think "movie"
- Think "Life"
- Think "pastry"
- Think "milk and eggs"
- Think "hot dog"
- Think "crisp baked good"
- Think "Japan"

Arrange the circled letters to solve the mystery answer.

MYSTERY ANSWER

ELEMENTS

JUMBLE BrainBusters!

Unscramble the Jumbles, one letter to each square, to spell names of elements.

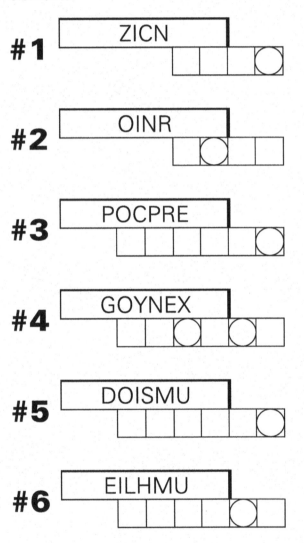

#1 ZICN

#2 OINR

THE PERIODIC TABLE

#3 POCPRE

#4 GOYNEX

Box of Clues

Stumped? Maybe you can find a clue below.

-Starts with "M"; ends with "Y"

-Starts with "I"; ends with "N"

-Starts with "C"; ends with "R"

-Starts with "H"; ends with "M"

-Starts with "O"; ends with "N"

-Starts with "S"; ends with "M"

-Starts with "Z"; ends with "C"

#5 DOISMU

#6 EILHMU

Arrange the circled letters to solve the mystery answer.

MYSTERY ANSWER

HEALTH & FITNESS

JUMBLE.
BrainBusters!

Unscramble the Jumbles, one letter to each square, to spell words related to health and fitness.

#1 WKLA

#2 OTRSGN

#3 REEYGN

#4 GEIWTH

#5 ESULMC

#6 BEOAICR

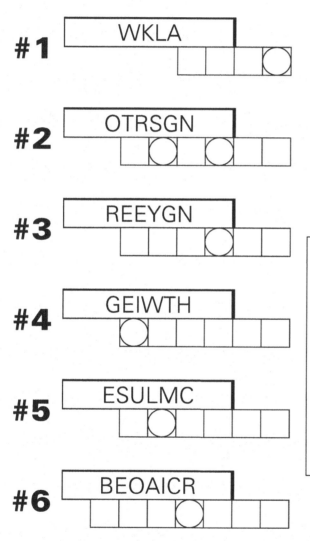

Interesting Health Facts

A healthy male should have about 12 to 15 percent body fat. A healthy woman should have between 15 to 18 percent.

Obesity is defined as 30 pounds or more over weight.

Arrange the circled letters to solve the mystery answer.

MYSTERY ANSWER

EUROPEAN COUNTRIES

JUMBLE
BrainBusters!

Unscramble the Jumbles, one letter to each square, to spell names of European countries.

#1 ANYROW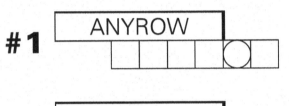

#2 ARELDIN

#3 AURKNIE

#4 AORNIAM

#5 GHNURAY

#6 AROUPTLG

Box of Clues

Stumped? Maybe you can find a clue below. (No clue for the Mystery Answer.)

- Home to Limerick
- Home to Budapest
- Spain's neighbor
- Home to Bucharest
- Sweden's neighbor
- Home to Kiev

Arrange the circled letters to solve the mystery answer.

MYSTERY ANSWER

PLANET EARTH

Unscramble the Jumbles, one letter to each square, to spell words related to planet Earth.

#1 CABHE

#2 NAILDS

#3 RTNUAD

#4 RACVNE

#5 GLONOA

#6 APTAUEL

Arrange the circled letters to solve the mystery answer.

★ JUMBLE® Trivia Quick Quiz

What might you be holding, if you were holding a substance that makes up about 12 percent of the Earth's surface?

MAUILMNU

ANSWER:

MYSTERY ANSWER

WEATHER

JUMBLE BrainBusters!

Unscramble the Jumbles, one letter to each square, to spell words related to weather.

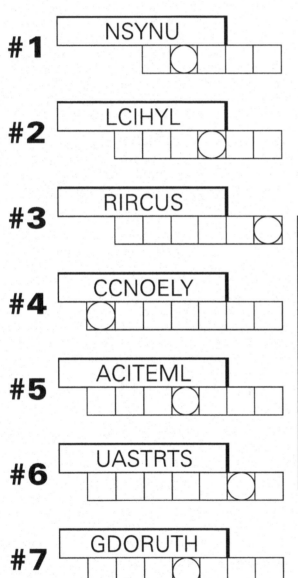

#1 NSYNU

#2 LCIHYL

#3 RIRCUS

#4 CCNOELY

#5 ACITEML

#6 UASTRTS

#7 GDORUTH

Interesting Weather Facts

Vanguard II was the first satellite to send weather information back to Earth from space (1959).

The 1995 United States heat wave contributed to more deaths in the U.S. than all other natural disasters put together.

Arrange the circled letters to solve the mystery answer.

MYSTERY ANSWER

PRESENTS

Unscramble the Jumbles, one letter to each square, to spell last names of U.S. presidents.

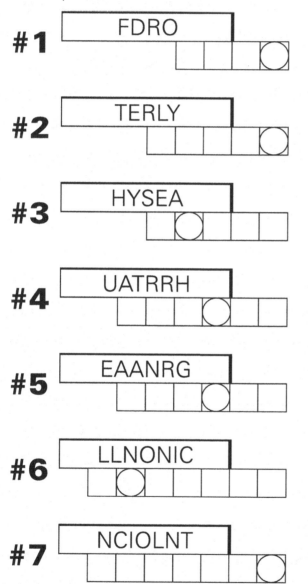

#1 FDRO

#2 TERLY

#3 HYSEA

#4 UATRRH

#5 EAANRG

#6 LLNONIC

#7 NCIOLNT

Mystery Answer Facts

-His middle name was Gamaliel
-He died in 1923
-He was born in Ohio
-He served as lieutenant governor of Ohio before becoming U.S. president

Arrange the circled letters to solve the mystery answer.

MYSTERY ANSWER

AFRICAN COUNTRIES

Unscramble the Jumbles, one letter to each square, to spell names of African countries.

#1 BLIAY

#2 EKYAN

#3 AZIABM

#4 ARDAWN

#5 ELIABIR

#6 COORMOC

Box of Clues

Stumped? Maybe you can find a clue below. (No clue for the Mystery Answer.)

-Starts with "Z"; ends with "A"
-Starts with "K"; ends with "A"
-Starts with "R"; ends with "A"
-Starts with "L"; ends with "A"
-Starts with "M"; ends with "O"
-Starts with "L"; ends with "A"

Arrange the circled letters to solve the mystery answer.

MYSTERY ANSWER

FOOD

Unscramble the Jumbles, one letter to each square, to spell words related to food.

#1 RIFTU

#2 LAEPP

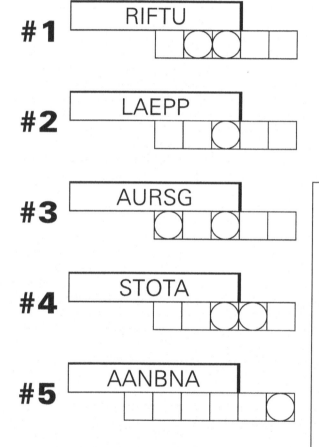

#3 AURSG

Interesting Food Facts

The Popsicle was invented in the early 1900s.

#4 STOTA

Haggis, a traditional Scottish dish, is made from the heart, lungs and liver of a sheep.

#5 AANBNA

The potato was considered an evil food in early Europe.

#6 FOEASOD

Arrange the circled letters to solve the mystery answer.

MYSTERY ANSWER

BIRDS

JUMBLE.
BrainBusters!

Unscramble the Jumbles, one letter to each square, to spell types of birds.

#1 OEDV

#2 GAEEL

#3 PFINFU

#4 GPIONE

#5 TORISHC

#6 RSARPWO

Interesting Bird Facts

Birds do not have sweat glands.

The Asian spine-tailed swift can fly at speeds of up to 100 mph.

Penguins have solid bones, unlike most birds, which have hollow bones.

Arrange the circled letters to solve the mystery answer.

MYSTERY ANSWER

PLANET EARTH

Unscramble the Jumbles, one letter to each square, to spell words related to planet Earth.

#1 URCTS

#2 AEWRT

#3 WSPMA

#4 ESSANO

#5 AGLERIC

#6 NOLAVOC

Interesting Planet Earth Facts

The Earth's orbit around the sun is slightly oval shaped.

The largest rain forest in the world is the Amazon rain forest in South America.

There are no rivers or lakes on Bermuda.

Arrange the circled letters to solve the mystery answer.

MYSTERY ANSWER

ELEMENTS

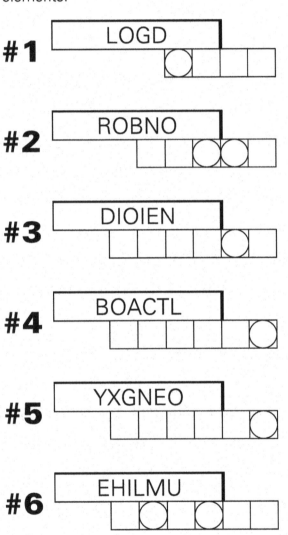

JUMBLE BrainBusters!

Unscramble the Jumbles, one letter to each square, to spell names of elements.

#1 LOGD

#2 ROBNO

#3 DIOIEN

#4 BOACTL

#5 YXGNEO

#6 EHILMU

THE PERIODIC TABLE

Box of Clues

Stumped? Maybe you can find a clue below.

-Starts with "C"; ends with "T"

-Starts with "B"; ends with "N"

-Starts with "N"; ends with "N"

-Starts with "G"; ends with "D"

-Starts with "I"; ends with "E"

-Starts with "O"; ends with "N"

-Starts with "H"; ends with "M"

Arrange the circled letters to solve the mystery answer.

MYSTERY ANSWER

AROUND THE HOME

JUMBLE BrainBusters!

Unscramble the Jumbles, one letter to each square, to spell words related to the home.

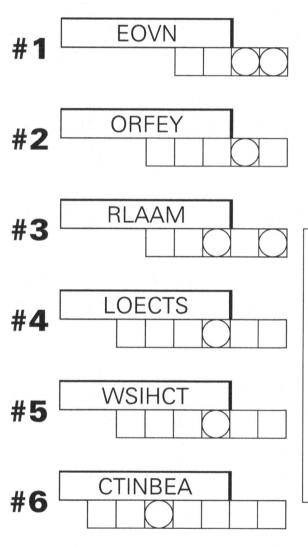

#1 EOVN

#2 ORFEY

#3 RLAAM

#4 LOECTS

#5 WSIHCT

#6 CTINBEA

Arrange the circled letters to solve the mystery answer.

Interesting Home Facts

The household refrigerator was patented in 1899.

A large percentage of household dust is made up of skin flakes.

The average dwelling in Japan has just under 1,000 square feet of living space.

MYSTERY ANSWER

FOOD

Unscramble the Jumbles, one letter to each square, to spell words related to food.

#1 AECK

#2 EHECSE

#3 UFIMFN

#4 FALWEF

#5 NPISCHA

#6 DUIPNGD

★ JUMBLE® Trivia Quick Quiz

What would you be eating if you were eating elbertas, redhavens, fairhavens and desert golds?

HEPCSEA

ANSWER:

Arrange the circled letters to solve the mystery answer.

MYSTERY ANSWER

THE HUMAN BODY

Unscramble the Jumbles, one letter to each square, to spell words related to the human body.

#1 UHBMT

#2 EPLSNE

#3 RHOTXA

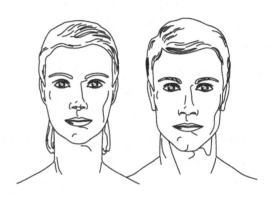

#4 RHYTIDO

#5 CTSMOHA

Interesting Human Body Facts

There are millions of digestive glands in the human stomach.

The human ear can distinguish from more than 1,000 musical tones.

There are billions of neurons in the human brain.

#6 BOAENDM

Arrange the circled letters to solve the mystery answer.

MYSTERY ANSWER

SPORTS

JUMBLE BrainBusters!

Unscramble the Jumbles, one letter to each square, to spell words related to sports.

#1 RRROE

#2 NCEHB

#3 PRIELT

#4 AGIELO

#5 FEEDESN

#6 RAAYIFW

★ **JUMBLE® Trivia** Quick Quiz

What might you have in your hand if you were holding something Americans spend more than $600 million a year on?

BOLAGLSFL

ANSWER:

Arrange the circled letters to solve the mystery answer.

MYSTERY ANSWER

TV SHOWS

JUMBLE
BrainBusters!

Unscramble the Jumbles, one letter to each square, to spell names of TV shows.

#1 SOCYB

#2 EHHEWA

#3 HRAIDEW

#4 ACTLKOM

#5 AHTESITN

#6 READJHON

Box of Clues

Stumped? Maybe you can find a clue below.

- Long-running syndicated show
- Popular ABC sitcom
- Bill's sitcom
- TV Western
- NBC legal drama set in Atlanta
- Judd Hirsch show 1988-1992
- Roger Moore show

Arrange the circled letters to solve the mystery answer.

MYSTERY ANSWER

OUTER SPACE

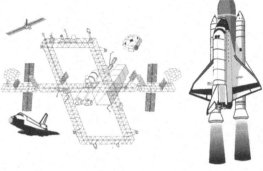

Unscramble the Jumbles, one letter to each square, to spell words related to outer space.

#1 ECOTM

#2 LAAYGX

#3 AURUSN

#4 SELCIEP

#5 TUIPJRE

#6 PNNEEUT

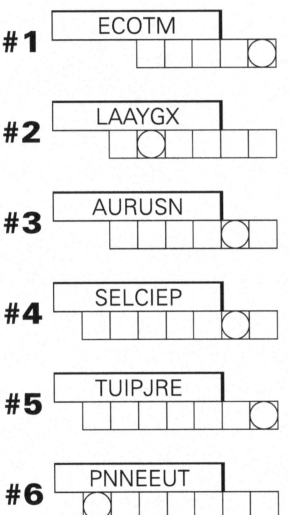

Interesting Outer Space Facts

At 60 miles per hour, it would take you 48 million years to drive to the nearest star (Proxima Centauri).

A typical galaxy has billions of stars.

If you weigh 200 pounds on Earth, you would weigh 76 pounds on Mars.

Arrange the circled letters to solve the mystery answer.

MYSTERY ANSWER

ANIMALS

JUMBLE BrainBusters!

Unscramble the Jumbles, one letter to each square, to spell names of animals.

#1 NIFHC

#2 YEHAN

#3 AALML

Box of Clues

Stumped? Maybe you can find a clue below. (No clue for the Mystery Answer.)

-Starts with "L"; ends with "A"
-Starts with "F"; ends with "T"
-Starts with "C"; ends with "R"
-Starts with "B"; ends with "T"
-Starts with "H"; ends with "A"
-Starts with "F"; ends with "H"

#4 RERFTE

#5 OABTCB

#6 AOCURG

Arrange the circled letters to solve the mystery answer.

MYSTERY ANSWER

POETRY

JUMBLE BrainBusters!

Unscramble the Jumbles, one letter to each square, to spell words found in the poem.

#1 YOSLLW

#2 CNIETO

#3 ZRAIEEL

#4 ARDBN

#5 CSODNE

#6 OBSCEEM

TIME by Kim Nolan

Minutes tick so _____ #1
Yet hours slip away
Before you even _____ #2
It's a whole new day

Weeks drag on forever
Yet months just disappear
Then you stop and _____ #3
It's a _____ #4 new year

Time is very clever
First slow then fast
It only takes a _____ #5
Then present _____ #6 past

Arrange the circled letters
to solve the mystery answer.
(The mystery answer is not
in the poem.)

MYSTERY ANSWER

U.S. STATE CAPITALS

Unscramble the Jumbles, one letter to each square, to spell names of U.S. state capitals.

#1 BSIEO

#2 TUAINS

#3 LLNOINC

#4 ARILGHE

#5 POYLIAM

#6 KAJCONS

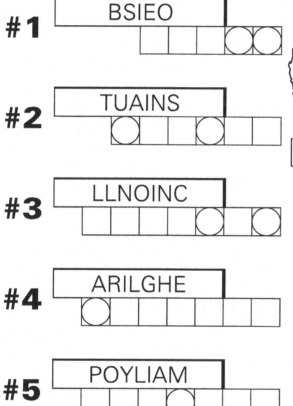

Box of Clues

Stumped? Maybe you can find a clue below.

- Capital of "The Lone Star State"
- Capital of "The Cornhusker State"
- Capital of "The Gem State"
- Capital of "The Golden State"
- Capital of "The Magnolia State"
- Capital of "The Chinook State"
- Capital of "The Tar Heel State"

Arrange the circled letters to solve the mystery answer.

MYSTERY ANSWER

ALL ABOUT MONEY

Unscramble the Jumbles, one letter to each square, to spell words related to money.

#1 LNAO

#2 AMKR

#3 AUTLV

#4 OTSKC

#5 UOPDN

#6 LALTEW

Box of Clues

Stumped? Maybe you can find a clue below. (No clue for the Mystery Answer.)

-German currency
-British currency
-Lent money
-Large storage area
-Small storage case
-_____ market

Arrange the circled letters to solve the mystery answer.

MYSTERY ANSWER

TV SHOWS

JUMBLE BrainBusters!

Unscramble the Jumbles, one letter to each square, to spell names of TV shows.

#1 AIECL

#2 AEGVS

#3 DAEUM

#4 LALDSA

#5 NNNOAC

#6 PFIELRP

Box of Clues

Stumped? Maybe you can find a clue below.

-Starts with "D"; ends with "S"

-Starts with "F"; ends with "R"

-Starts with "A"; ends with "E"

-Starts with "P"; ends with "E"

-Starts with "V"; ends with "S"

-Starts with "C"; ends with "N"

-Starts with "M"; ends with "E"

Arrange the circled letters to solve the mystery answer.

MYSTERY ANSWER

FAMOUS ATHLETES

Unscramble the Jumbles, one letter to each square, to spell names of famous athletes.

#1 KIGN

#2 LHUL

#3 AMISR

#4 RVEIGN

#5 ROJDNA

#6 AOMNNAT

Box of Clues

Stumped? Maybe you can find a clue below.

- Billie Jean _____
- Talented Bull
- Green New Yorker
- Yankee Roger
- Hockey Bobby
- Philadelphia's "Doctor"
- S.F. Joe

MYSTERY ANSWER

Arrange the circled letters to solve the mystery answer.

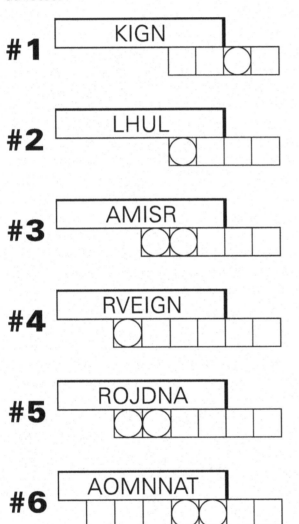

ANIMALS

JUMBLE. BrainBusters!

Unscramble the Jumbles, one letter to each square, to spell names of animals.

#1 ADPAN

#2 UKKNS

#3 ABEREV

#4 ECIKNHC

#5 TANREHP

#6 CEPCOKA

Mystery Answer Facts

-Ruminant mammal
-Genus Rangifer
-Found in arctic and subarctic regions
-Can travel 40 miles in one day
-Travels as part of a herd
-Feeds on plants and grasses

Arrange the circled letters to solve the mystery answer.

MYSTERY ANSWER

ACTORS & ACTRESSES

JUMBLE
BrainBusters!

Unscramble the Jumbles, one letter to each square, to spell the names of actors and actresses.

#1 OBREEKD

#2 ORBIENERR

#3 GUHRAGHNT

#4 ATTKHYBESA

#5 EANJURCTIN

#6 WOLOADLENY

Box of Clues

Stumped? Maybe you can find a clue below.

-Carl R.'s son
-Misery star
-Famous New Yorker
-Popular comedian, sitcom star
-Ex-Saturday Night Live star
-10 star, John D.'s wife
-Notting Hill star

Arrange the circled letters to solve the mystery answer.

MYSTERY ANSWER

THE HUMAN BODY

Unscramble the Jumbles, one letter to each square, to spell words related to the human body.

#1 KNELA

#2 OOTHT

#3 EUFRM

#4 UOTMH

#5 RTAYER

#6 RHTOTA

Box of Clues

Stumped? Maybe you can find a clue below. (No clue for the Mystery Answer.)

-Starts with "T"; ends with "H"
-Starts with "M"; ends with "H"
-Starts with "A"; ends with "Y"
-Starts with "F"; ends with "R"
-Starts with "T"; ends with "T"
-Starts with "A"; ends with "E"

Arrange the circled letters to solve the mystery answer.

MYSTERY ANSWER

ISLANDS

**JUMBLE.
BrainBusters!**

Unscramble the Jumbles, one letter to each square, to spell names of islands.

#1 RCPYUS

#2 RCSICOA

#3 AIELNCD

#4 CJMAIAA

#5 AABMASH

#6 DBREAUM

Box of Clues

Stumped? Maybe you can find a clue below. (No clue for the Mystery Answer.)

-Starts with "I", Ends with "D"
-Starts with "C", Ends with "S"
-Starts with "B", Ends with "A"
-Starts with "J", Ends with "A"
-Starts with "B", Ends with "S"
-Starts with "C", Ends with "A"

Arrange the circled letters to solve the mystery answer.

MYSTERY ANSWER

ANIMALS

Unscramble the Jumbles, one letter
to each square, to spell names of
animals.

#1 PIHOP

#2 NIFHC

#3 ALZDIR

#4 LTRUET

#5 RYTEKU

#6 FIRGFEA

#7 HCEICNK

JUMBLE® Trivia Quick Quiz

What type of animal
might you be looking at,
if you were looking at an
animal that could
produce just one calf
every five years?

LAETHNEP

ANSWER:

Arrange the circled letters
to solve the mystery answer.

MYSTERY ANSWER

HISTORIC PEOPLE

JUMBLE
BrainBusters!

Unscramble the Jumbles, one letter to each square, to spell last names of important people in history.

#1 RFUDE

#2 ANHGID

#3 ZORMTA

#4 NLLINOC

#5 PAOLONNE

#6 MOLCUUSB

Box of Clues

Stumped? Maybe you can find a clue below.

-French warrior
-Polish astronomer
-Austrian composer
-U.S. president
-Austrian psychologist
-Indian leader
-Famous explorer

Arrange the circled letters to solve the mystery answer.

MYSTERY ANSWER

AWARD-WINNING MOVIES

JUMBLE.
BrainBusters!

Unscramble the Jumbles, one letter
to each square, to spell titles of movies
that won "Best Picture" Oscar awards.

#1 KROYC

#2 AGNHID

#3 TAOPNT

Box of Clues

Stumped? Maybe you can find a
clue below.

-"Best Picture" 1970
-"Best Picture" 1982
-"Best Picture" 1976
-"Best Picture" 1997
-"Best Picture" 1988
-"Best Picture" 1973
-"Best Picture" 1986

#4 PALNOOT

#5 NAIARNM

#6 NHTGEIST

Arrange the circled letters
to solve the mystery answer.

MYSTERY ANSWER

U.S. CITIES

JUMBLE BrainBusters!

Unscramble the Jumbles, one letter to each square, to spell names of U.S. cities.

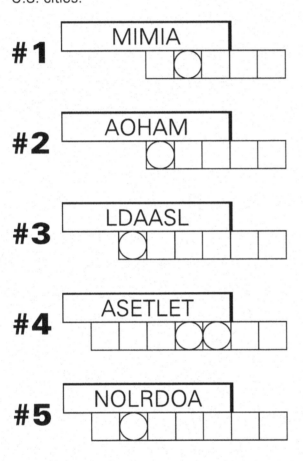

#1 MIMIA

#2 AOHAM

#3 LDAASL

#4 ASETLET

#5 NOLRDOA

#6 HMEMISP

Box of Clues

Stumped? Maybe you can find a clue below. (No clue for the Mystery Answer.)

-Large Texas city
-Nebraska city
-Inland Florida city
-Pacific Northwest city
-City on the Mississippi
-Florida coastal city

Arrange the circled letters to solve the mystery answer.

MYSTERY ANSWER

RIVERS

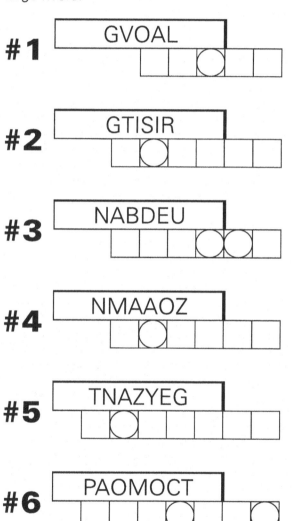

Unscramble the Jumbles, one letter to each square, to spell names of large rivers.

#1 GVOAL

#2 GTISIR

#3 NABDEU

#4 NMAAOZ

#5 TNAZYEG

#6 PAOMOCT

Box of Clues

Stumped? Maybe you can find a clue below.

- Starts with "D"; ends with "E"
- Starts with "A"; ends with "N"
- Starts with "P"; ends with "C"
- Starts with "C"; ends with "A"
- Starts with "T"; ends with "S"
- Starts with "V"; ends with "A"
- Starts with "Y"; ends with "E"

Arrange the circled letters to solve the mystery answer.

MYSTERY ANSWER

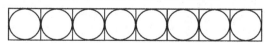

ALL ABOUT MUSIC

Unscramble the Jumbles, one letter to each square, to spell words related to music.

#1 NMIRO

#2 MEOTP

#3 LEOYMD

#4 THHRMY

#5 ATCNTAA

#6 GLAEOLR

Box of Clues

Stumped? Maybe you can find a clue below. (No clue for the Mystery Answer.)

-Starts with "R"; ends with "M"

-Starts with "A"; ends with "O"

-Starts with "C"; ends with "A"

-Starts with "T"; ends with "O"

-Starts with "M"; ends with "R"

-Starts with "M"; ends with "Y"

Arrange the circled letters to solve the mystery answer.

MYSTERY ANSWER

ANSWERS

1. **Jumbles:** #1. RHINO #2. EAGLE #3. SKUNK #4. MOUSE #5. WALRUS #6. RACCOON
   Answer: COUGAR

2. **Jumbles:** #1. TAXI #2. DALLAS #3. CHEERS #4. FRASIER #5. SPIN CITY #6. STAR TREK
   Answer: SEINFELD

3. **Jumbles:** #1. PIZZA #2. CANDY #3. DONUT #4. PICKLE #5. BURGER #6. KETCHUP
   Answer: PUDDING

4. **Jumbles:** #1. OHIO #2. IOWA #3. IDAHO #4. MAINE #5. KANSAS #6. VERMONT
   Answer: INDIANA

5. **Jumbles:** #1. COMET #2. SATURN #3. ECLIPSE #4. GRAVITY #5. NEPTUNE #6. MERCURY
   Answer: UNIVERSE

6. **Jumbles:** #1. CASH #2. VAULT #3. PENNY #4. FRANC #5. CHECK #6. INVEST
   Answer: INTEREST

7. **Jumbles:** #1. ALIEN #2. BRAZIL #3. CASINO #4. PATTON #5. PSYCHO #6. WITNESS
   Answer: CASABLANCA

8. **Jumbles:** #1. SHIRT #2. GLOVE #3. JACKET #4. SANDAL #5. MITTEN #6. SNEAKER
   Answer: GARMENT

9. **Jumbles:** #1. DAMP SOGGY #2. HARM DAMAGE #3. PRIZE AWARD #4. RAPID SPEEDY #5. LAUGH CACKLE #6. ERUPT EXPLODE
   Answer: HOME HOUSE

10. **Jumbles:** #1. GIFT #2. PRICE #3. CLERK #4. STORE #5. COUPON #6. BROWSE
    Answer: RECEIPT

11. **Jumbles:** #1. FOUL #2. PIVOT #3. BLOCK #4. BASKET #5. REFEREE #6. DEFENSE
    Answer: DRIBBLE

12. **Jumbles:** #1. MAINE #2. BOSTON #3. PILGRIM #4. VERMONT #5. CAPE COD #6. HARTFORD
    Answer: RHODE ISLAND

13. **Jumbles:** #1. HOOD #2. LIGHT #3. WHEEL #4. DRIVER #5. ENGINE #6. PICKUP
    Answer: VEHICLE

14. **Jumbles:** #1. MEXICO #2. ROCKIES #3. TIJUANA #4. SEATTLE #5. HOUSTON #6. TORONTO
    Answer: LAKE HURON

15. **Jumbles:** #1. TRAIN #2. EATING #3. MUSCLE #4. RUNNING #5. AEROBIC #6. STRENGTH
    Answer: CALORIES

16. **Jumbles:** #1. ZINC #2. COPPER #3. COBALT #4. SULFUR #5. HELIUM #6. SILICON
    Answer: CHLORINE

17. **Jumbles:** #1. NECK #2. JOINT #3. BRAIN #4. ANKLE #5. CHEST #6. PELVIS
    Answer: SKELETON

18. **Jumbles:** #1. FOUL #2. TRACK #3. COACH #4. LEAGUE #5. BASKET #6. FUMBLE
    Answer: SOFTBALL

19. **Jumbles:** #1. ED HARRIS #2. JIM CARREY #3. DEMI MOORE #4. JOHNNY DEPP #5. GOLDIE HAWN #6. TOM SELLECK
    Answer: AL PACINO

20. **Jumbles:** #1. CHILE #2. BRAZIL #3. MEXICO #4. SWEDEN #5. PANAMA #6. IRELAND #7. AUSTRIA
    Answer: THAILAND

21. **Jumbles:** #1. SEED #2. FERN #3. GRASS #4. BLOOM #5. NEEDLE #6. ORCHID #7. BAMBOO
    Answer: FOLIAGE

22. **Jumbles:** #1. FRANCE #2. SWEDEN #3. IRELAND #4. AUSTRIA #5. ENGLAND #6. BELGIUM
    Answer: GREECE

23. **Jumbles:** #1. TIGER #2. CANNON #3. JUGGLER #4. TRAPEZE #5. ACROBAT
    Answer: ARENA

24. **Jumbles:** #1. SLICK #2. ROUGH #3. BOGEY #4. WEDGE #5. DRIVER #6. PUTTER
    Answer: TIGER WOODS

25. **Jumbles:** #1. CAIRO #2. BERLIN #3. SYDNEY #4. MADRID #5. BOMBAY #6. TORONTO
    Answer: LONDON

26. **Jumbles:** #1. FAIR #2. DAMP #3. FRONT #4. FLOOD #5. CLOUDY #6. FREEZE
    Answer: RAINFALL

27. **Jumbles:** #1. HARP #2. FLUTE #3. BANJO #4. GUITAR #5. PICCOLO #6. TRUMPET
    Answer: CLARINET

28. **Jumbles:** #1. POLK #2. HAYES #3. GRANT #4. ADAMS #5. CLINTON #6. JACKSON
    Answer: JOHNSON

29. **Jumbles:** #1. HIPPO #2. CAMEL #3. ZEBRA #4. GOPHER #5. GIRAFFE #6. BUFFALO #7. KANGAROO
    Answer: PORCUPINE

30. **Jumbles:** #1. HAWK #2. WREN #3. CROW #4. STORK #5. PIGEON #6. CANARY
    Answer: SPARROW

31. **Jumbles:** #1. HOWE #2. BRETT #3. BERRA #4. BROWN #5. NAMATH #6. GIFFORD
    Answer: BEN HOGAN

32. **Jumbles: #1.** CABIN **#2.** FLAPS **#3.** ENGINE **#4.** RUDDER **#5.** AIRFOIL
Answer: FUSELAGE

33. **Jumbles: #1.** HAIR **#2.** BRAIN **#3.** BLOOD **#4.** ANKLE **#5.** TOOTH **#6.** MUSCLE **#7.** EARDRUM
Answer: BACKBONE

34. **Jumbles: #1.** THROUGH **#2.** CHILDREN **#3.** UPTOWN **#4.** PEOPLE **#5.** HOME **#6.** APPEAR **#7.** WINTER
Answer: WINTERTIME

35. **Jumbles: #1.** TEST **#2.** TARDY **#3.** EXPEL **#4.** LUNCH **#5.** ANSWER **#6.** SCIENCE
Answer: CLASSES
Quick Quiz Answer: HARVARD

36. **Jumbles: #1.** SIX + SIX = TWELVE
#2. TWO × FOUR = EIGHT
#3. FIVE + ONE + ONE = SEVEN
#4. TWELVE ÷ FOUR = THREE
#5. TWO + FOUR = THREE × TWO
Answer: TWO × TWO = SIXTEEN ÷ FOUR

37. **Jumbles: #1.** BEACH **#2.** TAMPA **#3.** MIAMI **#4.** ORANGE **#5.** ORLANDO **#6.** SUNSHINE
Answer: PENINSULA

38. **Jumbles: #1.** CATCH **#2.** GLOVE **#3.** INNING **#4.** STRIKE **#5.** BOXING **#6.** RUNNER
Answer: TENNIS

39. **Jumbles: #1.** EGGS **#2.** APPLE **#3.** CHERRY **#4.** POTATO **#5.** MUFFIN **#6.** WAFFLE
Answer: SPAGHETTI
Quick Quiz Answer: POTATO CHIPS

40. **Jumbles: #1.** WALL **#2.** LIGHT **#3.** CHAIR **#4.** FLOOR **#5.** OUTLET **#6.** CEILING
Answer: GARAGE

41. **Jumbles: #1.** BOISE **#2.** ALBANY **#3.** LANSING **#4.** PHOENIX **#5.** ATLANTA **#6.** JACKSON
Answer: LINCOLN

42. **Jumbles: #1.** PILOT **#2.** AUTHOR **#3.** BARBER **#4.** DOCTOR **#5.** JANITOR **#6.** PLUMBER
Answer: REALTOR

43. **Jumbles: #1.** DUBLIN **#2.** LONDON **#3.** LISBON **#4.** MADRID **#5.** VIENNA **#6.** WARSAW
Answer: BERLIN

44. **Jumbles: #1.** OBOE **#2.** PIANO **#3.** CHORD **#4.** MAJOR **#5.** TEMPO **#6.** GUITAR
Answer: TRUMPET

45. **Jumbles: #1.** SLUSH **#2.** FLOOD **#3.** HUMID **#4.** WINDY **#5.** STORM **#6.** DEGREE **#7.** TWISTER
Answer: THUNDER

46. **Jumbles: #1.** INDIA **#2.** TURKEY **#3.** ICELAND **#4.** FINLAND **#5.** HUNGARY **#6.** ROMANIA
Answer: LITHUANIA

47. **Jumbles: #1.** RIVER **#2.** BEACH **#3.** CRUST **#4.** SWAMP **#5.** ISLAND **#6.** GEYSER
Answer: GLACIER

48. **Jumbles: #1.** APRIL **#2.** CABIN **#3.** SPEECH **#4.** LAWYER **#5.** DEBATE **#6.** KENTUCKY
Answer: PRESIDENT

49. **Jumbles: #1.** ROBIN **#2.** EAGLE **#3.** STORK **#4.** PENGUIN **#5.** PEACOCK **#6.** BUZZARD
Answer: CARDINAL

50. **Jumbles: #1.** IRON **#2.** SULFUR **#3.** COBALT **#4.** HELIUM **#5.** SILICON **#6.** MERCURY
Answer: URANIUM

51. **Jumbles: #1.** BRICK **#2.** CHAIR **#3.** TABLE **#4.** PHONE **#5.** PORCH **#6.** CARPET
Answer: CABINET

52. **Jumbles: #1.** BOOT **#2.** PARKA **#3.** FABRIC **#4.** OUTFIT **#5.** BUTTON **#6.** MITTEN
Answer: UNIFORM

53. **Jumbles: #1.** BEEF **#2.** SNACK **#3.** COOKIE **#4.** WAFFLE **#5.** PRETZEL **#6.** OATMEAL
Answer: MEAT LOAF

54. **Jumbles: #1.** PUTTER **#2.** TROPHY **#3.** DEFEAT **#4.** SEASON **#5.** FENCING **#6.** ARCHERY
Answer: OPPONENT
Quick Quiz Answer: BADMINTON

55. **Jumbles: #1.** AUSTIN **#2.** HELENA **#3.** BOSTON **#4.** RALEIGH **#5.** AUGUSTA **#6.** CONCORD
Answer: HONOLULU

56. **Jumbles: #1.** LUNG **#2.** HEAD **#3.** COLON **#4.** TOOTH **#5.** THUMB **#6.** THROAT
Answer: TONGUE

57. **Jumbles: #1.** FRENCH **#2.** OTTAWA **#3.** CALGARY **#4.** PROVINCE **#5.** MANITOBA **#6.** MONTREAL
Answer: TORONTO

58. **Jumbles: #1.** CREEK **#2.** PUEBLO **#3.** MOJAVE **#4.** MOHAWK **#5.** SEMINOLE **#6.** CHEYENNE
Answer: COMANCHE

59. **Jumbles: #1.** ANTZ **#2.** GANDHI **#3.** PLATOON **#4.** RAIN MAN **#5.** THE BIRDS **#6.** TOY STORY
Answer: HIGH NOON

60. **Jumbles: #1.** BORG **#2.** LOUIS **#3.** BENCH **#4.** PAYTON **#5.** JORDAN **#6.** FOREMAN
Answer: LARRY BIRD

61. **Jumbles: #1.** ORBIT **#2.** COMET **#3.** URANUS **#4.** JUPITER **#5.** NEPTUNE **#6.** MERCURY
Answer: METEORITE
Quick Quiz Answer: APPLESAUCE

62. **Jumbles: #1.** MINT **#2.** VALUE **#3.** STOCK **#4.** POUND **#5.** CHARGE **#6.** DOLLAR
Answer: RECEIPT

63. **Jumbles: #1.** HAND **#2.** BRAIN **#3.** GLAND **#4.** COLON **#5.** BLOOD **#6.** TONGUE
Answer: BLADDER

64. **Jumbles: #1.** PROP **#2.** STUNT **#3.** SCRIPT **#4.** STUDIO **#5.** WRITER **#6.** CAMERA
Answer: COSTUME
Quick Quiz Answer: MY FAIR LADY

65. **Jumbles: #1.** RADIO **#2.** TRUNK **#3.** GAUGE **#4.** WIPER **#5.** ALARM **#6.** ENGINE
Answer: GARAGE

66. **Jumbles: #1.** PANDA **#2.** CHIMP **#3.** TURTLE **#4.** COYOTE **#5.** GOPHER **#6.** VULTURE
Answer: CROCODILE

67. **Jumbles: #1.** SOCK **#2.** STYLE **#3.** TAILOR **#4.** FABRIC **#5.** VELVET **#6.** BUTTON
Answer: NECKLACE

68. **Jumbles: #1.** COACH **#2.** TRIPLE **#3.** SINGLE **#4.** DOUBLE **#5.** WALKED **#6.** CATCHER
Answer: WILD PITCH
Quick Quiz Answer: RED BARBER

69. **Jumbles: #1.** RICH POOR **#2.** FULL EMPTY **#3.** SAFE RISKY **#4.** GROW SHRINK **#5.** BASE SUMMIT **#6.** CHEER GLOOM
Answer: PLUS MINUS

70. **Jumbles: #1.** SICK **#2.** CURE **#3.** CLINIC **#4.** HEALTH **#5.** SURGEON **#6.** HOSPITAL
Answer: ILLNESS

71. **Jumbles: #1.** TAFT **#2.** FORD **#3.** NIXON **#4.** HOOVER **#5.** WILSON **#6.** JOHNSON
Answer: HARRISON
Quick Quiz Answer: RONALD REAGAN

72. **Jumbles: #1.** FLUTE **#2.** VIOLIN **#3.** FINALE **#4.** GUITAR **#5.** RHYTHM **#6.** MELODY
Answer: OVERTURE
Quick Quiz Answer: WARREN BEATTY

73. **Jumbles: #1.** VIENNA **#2.** DUBLIN **#3.** HAVANA **#4.** MOSCOW **#5.** CARACAS **#6.** BRUSSELS
Answer: LISBON

74. **Jumbles: #1.** TAILOR **#2.** BUTLER **#3.** BROKER **#4.** CASHIER **#5.** SURGEON **#6.** JEWELER
Answer: WAITER

75. **Jumbles: #1.** WARM **#2.** RADAR **#3.** STORM **#4.** COOLER **#5.** BREEZE **#6.** RAINBOW **#7.** MONSOON
Answer: BAROMETER
Quick Quiz Answer: ENGLAND

76. **Jumbles: #1.** CATCH **#2.** BLOCK **#3.** TACKLE **#4.** FUMBLE **#5.** KICKOFF **#6.** PENALTY
Answer: HALFTIME
Quick Quiz Answer: INSTANT REPLAY

77. **Jumbles: #1.** TENT **#2.** SHOW **#3.** CLOWN **#4.** TRAPEZE **#5.** ACROBAT
Answer: ELEPHANT

78. **Jumbles: #1.** INDIA **#2.** SYRIA **#3.** RUSSIA **#4.** VIETNAM **#5.** PAKISTAN **#6.** MONGOLIA
Answer: SINGAPORE

79. **Jumbles: #1.** LION **#2.** TIGER **#3.** HYENA **#4.** JACKAL **#5.** BADGER **#6.** GRIZZLY **#7.** LEOPARD
Answer: POLAR BEAR

80. **Jumbles: #1.** TRAIN **#2.** YACHT **#3.** TRUCK **#4.** BLIMP **#5.** SUBWAY **#6.** BICYCLE
Answer: AIRPLANE

81. **Jumbles: #1.** CAVE **#2.** WATER **#3.** JUNGLE **#4.** VALLEY **#5.** TUNDRA **#6.** LAGOON
Answer: VOLCANO

82. **Jumbles: #1.** TWO + TWO = FOUR **#2.** ONE + SEVEN = EIGHT **#3.** FOUR × FOUR = SIXTEEN **#4.** ONE + FOUR = FIVE × ONE **#5.** EIGHT + TWO = TEN + ZERO
Answer: ONE × ONE = THREE – THREE + ONE

83. **Jumbles: #1.** HAWAII **#2.** NEVADA **#3.** OREGON **#4.** FLORIDA **#5.** ARIZONA **#6.** KENTUCKY
Answer: COLORADO
Quick Quiz Answer: LOUISIANA

84. **Jumbles: #1.** MATH **#2.** DUNCE **#3.** PENCIL **#4.** LOCKER **#5.** LIBRARY **#6.** COLLEGE
Answer: DIPLOMA

85. **Jumbles: #1.** FULL HOUSE **#2.** EMPTY NEST **#3.** GOOD TIMES **#4.** I LOVE LUCY **#5.** FAMILY TIES **#6.** GREEN ACRES
Answer: MISTER ED

86. **Jumbles: #1.** FRENCH **#2.** MARTHA **#3.** VICTORY **#4.** COUNTRY **#5.** VIRGINIA **#6.** DELAWARE
Answer: MOUNT VERNON

87. **Jumbles: #1.** GULL **#2.** FINCH **#3.** GOOSE **#4.** OSPREY **#5.** TURKEY **#6.** CHICKEN
Answer: CUCKOO

88. **Jumbles: #1.** CHILE **#2.** RIVER **#3.** BRAZIL **#4.** AMAZON **#5.** BOLIVIA **#6.** ECUADOR
Answer: COLOMBIA

89. **Jumbles: #1.** ALGAE **#2.** WOODS **#3.** ORCHID **#4.** POLLEN **#5.** BRANCH **#6.** FLOWER
Answer: SEEDLING

90. **Jumbles: #1.** POLK **#2.** GRANT **#3.** TAYLOR **#4.** HOOVER **#5.** HARDING **#6.** JACKSON
Answer: LINCOLN

91. **Jumbles: #1.** CHILE **#2.** SYRIA **#3.** KENYA **#4.** RUSSIA **#5.** JORDAN **#6.** MEXICO **#7.** IRELAND
Answer: SOMALIA

92. **Jumbles: #1.** FLAKE **#2.** FOGGY **#3.** WINDY **#4.** CHILLY **#5.** DEGREE **#6.** THUNDER
Answer: LIGHTNING
Quick Quiz Answer: PUERTO RICO

93. **Jumbles: #1.** OBOE **#2.** DRUM **#3.** FLUTE **#4.** VIOLIN **#5.** CORNET **#6.** BASSOON
Answer: TROMBONE

94. **Jumbles: #1.** BLUFF **#2.** ABYSS **#3.** GLOBE **#4.** GEYSER **#5.** LAGOON **#6.** SURFACE
Answer: GEOLOGY

95. **Jumbles: #1.** POLAND **#2.** NORWAY **#3.** FINLAND **#4.** ENGLAND **#5.** HUNGARY **#6.** GERMANY
Answer: ROMANIA

96. **Jumbles: #1.** WINE **#2.** TAHOE **#3.** VALLEY **#4.** FRESNO **#5.** CASCADES **#6.** YOSEMITE
Answer: SACRAMENTO

97. **Jumbles: #1.** ENERGY **#2.** MATTER **#3.** NEWTON **#4.** ANALYZE **#5.** ELEMENT **#6.** COMPOUND
Answer: ANATOMY

98. **Jumbles: #1.** FIGHT **#2.** ERROR **#3.** HOMER **#4.** INNING **#5.** HOCKEY **#6.** DUGOUT
Answer: UNIFORM

99. **Jumbles: #1.** ALBANY **#2.** JUNEAU **#3.** TOPEKA **#4.** LINCOLN **#5.** LANSING **#6.** PHOENIX
Answer: JACKSON
Quick Quiz Answer: TALLAHASSEE

100. **Jumbles: #1.** MEG RYAN **#2.** MAE WEST **#3.** TOM HANKS **#4.** VAL KILMER **#5.** MEL GIBSON **#6.** TOM CRUISE
Answer: ROBIN WILLIAMS

101. **Jumbles: #1.** DONUT **#2.** COOKIE **#3.** PEPPER **#4.** BUTTER **#5.** CEREAL **#6.** MUFFIN
Answer: POPCORN

102. **Jumbles: #1.** ARCTIC **#2.** CANADA **#3.** ROCKIES **#4.** CHICAGO **#5.** BUFFALO **#6.** MONTREAL
Answer: CALIFORNIA

103. **Jumbles: #1.** CUBA **#2.** FARGO **#3.** THE FIRM **#4.** FANTASIA **#5.** GODZILLA **#6.** MAGNOLIA
Answer: SLING BLADE

104. **Jumbles: #1.** TAMPA **#2.** MOBILE **#3.** DETROIT **#4.** CHICAGO **#5.** ATLANTA **#6.** HOUSTON
Answer: SEATTLE

105. **Jumbles: #1.** COACH **#2.** ZORRO **#3.** MANNIX **#4.** BENSON **#5.** DYNASTY **#6.** ROSEANNE
Answer: BONANZA

106. **Jumbles: #1.** DEBATE **#2.** ENSLAVE **#3.** MIGHT **#4.** FIGHT **#5.** FUMBLE **#6.** JUMBLE
Answer: LANGUAGE

107. **Jumbles: #1.** GLAND **#2.** FIBULA **#3.** KIDNEY **#4.** THORAX **#5.** MUSCLE **#6.** ENAMEL
Answer: LIGAMENT
Quick Quiz Answer: TEMPORAL LOBE

108. **Jumbles: #1.** RUGBY **#2.** BLOCK **#3.** CATCH **#4.** BASKET **#5.** FUMBLE **#6.** DRIBBLE
Answer: BASEBALL

109. **Jumbles: #1.** ORBIT **#2.** LUNAR **#3.** PLUTO **#4.** APOLLO **#5.** JUPITER **#6.** SHUTTLE
Answer: SATELLITE

110. **Jumbles: #1.** HOTEL **#2.** CANNON **#3.** MATLOCK **#4.** NEWHART **#5.** WEBSTER **#6.** LOU GRANT
Answer: HUNTER

111. **Jumbles: #1.** KODIAK **#2.** TUNDRA **#3.** VALDEZ **#4.** JUNEAU **#5.** GLACIER **#6.** MCKINLEY
Answer: YUKON RIVER

112. **Jumbles: #1.** SPLASH **#2.** HAVANA **#3.** DIE HARD **#4.** SCARFACE **#5.** CITY HALL **#6.** THE STING
Answer: THE SHINING

113. **Jumbles: #1.** NAVAJO **#2.** APACHE **#3.** ARAPAHO **#4.** MOHICAN **#5.** SHAWNEE **#6.** CHEROKEE
Answer: CHICKASAW

114. **Jumbles: #1.** KOALA **#2.** PERTH **#3.** WOMBAT **#4.** WALLABY **#5.** PLATYPUS **#6.** CANBERRA
Answer: MELBOURNE

115. **Jumbles: #1.** MEL GIBSON **#2.** RENE RUSSO **#3.** AMY IRVING **#4.** JAMES CAAN **#5.** JOHN CUSACK **#6.** KATHY BATES
Answer: JULIA ROBERTS

116. **Jumbles: #1.** TIGER **#2.** JACKAL **#3.** BABOON **#4.** PENGUIN **#5.** CHEETAH **#6.** MUSKRAT
Answer: CHIPMUNK
Quick Quiz Answer: CHAMELEON

117. **Jumbles: #1.** TABLE **#2.** FRAME **#3.** OUTLET **#4.** PANTRY **#5.** GARAGE **#6.** WINDOW
Answer: PLUMBING

118. **Jumbles: #1.** LOON **#2.** FINCH **#3.** RAVEN **#4.** MACAW **#5.** PENGUIN **#6.** VULTURE
Answer: FLAMINGO

119. **Jumbles: #1.** NYLON **#2.** DRESS **#3.** JEANS **#4.** APPAREL **#5.** SWEATER **#6.** GARMENT
Answer: JEWELRY

120. **Jumbles: #1.** TRUCK **#2.** TRUNK **#3.** WIPER **#4.** PICKUP **#5.** BUMPER **#6.** EXHAUST
Answer: MECHANIC

121. **Jumbles: #1.** POLKA **#2.** ETUDE **#3.** OPERA **#4.** CHORD **#5.** LEGATO **#6.** SONATA
Answer: ALLEGRO

122. **Jumbles: #1.** HAIL **#2.** ICICLE **#3.** ISOBAR **#4.** DEGREE **#5.** CLOUDY **#6.** NIMBUS
Answer: CYCLONE

123. **Jumbles: #1.** BOXER **#2.** HOUND **#3.** HUSKY **#4.** BEAGLE **#5.** SPANIEL **#6.** BULLDOG **#7.** DOBERMAN
Answer: GREYHOUND

124. **Jumbles: #1.** HARRY **#2.** GEORGE **#3.** GROVER **#4.** MARTIN **#5.** DWIGHT **#6.** HERBERT
Answer: THEODORE

125. **Jumbles: #1.** TWO − TWO = ZERO **#2.** ONE + THREE = FOUR **#3.** FIVE + TWO = SEVEN **#4.** ONE + NINE − ONE = NINE **#5.** TEN − FOUR = THREE + THREE
Answer: ONE + ONE − ZERO = FIVE − THREE

126. **Jumbles: #1.** BRAZIL **#2.** GREECE **#3.** SWEDEN **#4.** AUSTRIA **#5.** JAMAICA **#6.** BELGIUM
Answer: AUSTRALIA
Quick Quiz Answer: PORTUGAL

127. **Jumbles: #1.** ARUBA **#2.** MALTA **#3.** SICILY **#4.** TAIWAN **#5.** ANTIGUA **#6.** BERMUDA
Answer: ICELAND

128. **Jumbles: #1.** PLANT **#2.** PRUNE **#3.** HUMUS **#4.** SHOVEL **#5.** FLOWER **#6.** COMPOST
Answer: HARVEST

129. **Jumbles: #1.** AUTRY **#2.** FIELDS **#3.** MARTIN **#4.** BURTON **#5.** COOPER **#6.** MATTHAU
Answer: MITCHUM

130. **Jumbles: #1.** TREE **#2.** LIGHT **#3.** TRUNK **#4.** WATER **#5.** BOTANY **#6.** CACTUS
Answer: THICKET

131. **Jumbles: #1.** BRAZIL **#2.** BOLIVIA **#3.** PACIFIC **#4.** URUGUAY **#5.** CARACAS **#6.** ATLANTIC
Answer: SANTIAGO

132. **Jumbles: #1.** SOAP **#2.** KOJAK **#3.** FAMILY **#4.** KUNG FU **#5.** DYNASTY **#6.** BARETTA
Answer: GUNSMOKE

133. **Jumbles: #1.** PIERRE **#2.** TOPEKA **#3.** BOSTON **#4.** RALEIGH **#5.** OLYMPIA **#6.** ATLANTA
Answer: TRENTON

134. **Jumbles: #1.** BASE **#2.** ALLEY **#3.** KICKER **#4.** BOXING **#5.** DEFENSE **#6.** STADIUM
Answer: BASKETBALL

135. **Jumbles: #1.** JAWS **#2.** GLORY **#3.** CON AIR **#4.** VERTIGO **#5.** MICHAEL **#6.** STAR WARS
Answer: CAST AWAY

136. **Jumbles: #1.** DALLAS **#2.** DETROIT **#3.** CHICAGO **#4.** ATLANTA **#5.** OAKLAND **#6.** BUFFALO
Answer: ORLANDO

137. **Jumbles: #1.** BANK **#2.** DEBIT **#3.** CHARGE **#4.** RECEIPT **#5.** ACCOUNT **#6.** PAYMENT
Answer: CURRENCY

138. **Jumbles: #1.** HYENA **#2.** GOOSE **#3.** LEMUR **#4.** MOOSE **#5.** PIGEON **#6.** GOPHER **#7.** GORILLA
Answer: LEMMING

139. **Jumbles: #1.** BIRD **#2.** AUSTIN **#3.** AGASSI **#4.** GEHRIG **#5.** BUTKUS **#6.** NELSON
Answer: HANK AARON

140. **Jumbles: #1.** MAINE **#2.** ALASKA **#3.** OREGON **#4.** GEORGIA **#5.** MONTANA **#6.** NEBRASKA
Answer: TENNESSEE

141. **Jumbles: #1.** NIXON **#2.** ADAMS **#3.** REAGAN **#4.** WILSON **#5.** CLINTON **#6.** JOHNSON
Answer: COOLIDGE

142. **Jumbles: #1.** MATH **#2.** LEARN **#3.** FLUNK **#4.** JUNIOR **#5.** MASCOT **#6.** HISTORY
Answer: FRESHMAN
Quick Quiz Answer: PRINCETON

143. **Jumbles: #1.** MAUDE **#2.** NURSES **#3.** WORKING **#4.** NEWHART **#5.** BLOSSOM **#6.** SEINFELD
Answer: FRASIER

144. **Jumbles: #1.** SUSHI **#2.** RELISH **#3.** DANISH **#4.** CEREAL **#5.** BISCUIT **#6.** POPCORN
Answer: CUSTARD

145. **Jumbles: #1.** ZINC **#2.** IRON **#3.** COPPER **#4.** OXYGEN **#5.** SODIUM **#6.** HELIUM
Answer: MERCURY

146. **Jumbles: #1.** WALK **#2.** STRONG **#3.** ENERGY **#4.** WEIGHT **#5.** MUSCLE **#6.** AEROBIC
Answer: WORKOUT

147. **Jumbles: #1.** NORWAY **#2.** IRELAND **#3.** UKRAINE **#4.** ROMANIA **#5.** HUNGARY **#6.** PORTUGAL
Answer: LITHUANIA

148. **Jumbles: #1.** BEACH **#2.** ISLAND
#3. TUNDRA **#4.** CAVERN **#5.** LAGOON
#6. PLATEAU
Answer: CONTINENT
Quick Quiz Answer: ALUMINUM

149. **Jumbles: #1.** SUNNY **#2.** CHILLY
#3. CIRRUS **#4.** CYCLONE **#5.** CLIMATE
#6. STRATUS **#7.** DROUGHT
Answer: CUMULUS

150. **Jumbles: #1.** FORD **#2.** TYLER **#3.** HAYES
#4. ARTHUR **#5.** REAGAN **#6.** LINCOLN
#7. CLINTON
Answer: HARDING

151. **Jumbles: #1.** LIBYA **#2.** KENYA **#3.** ZAMBIA
#4. RWANDA **#5.** LIBERIA **#6.** MOROCCO
Answer: ZIMBABWE

152. **Jumbles: #1.** FRUIT **#2.** APPLE **#3.** SUGAR
#4. TOAST **#5.** BANANA **#6.** SEAFOOD
Answer: ASPARAGUS

153. **Jumbles: #1.** DOVE **#2.** EAGLE **#3.** PUFFIN
#4. PIGEON **#5.** OSTRICH **#6.** SPARROW
Answer: PARTRIDGE

154. **Jumbles: #1.** CRUST **#2.** WATER
#3. SWAMP **#4.** SEASON **#5.** GLACIER
#6. VOLCANO
Answer: CLIMATE

155. **Jumbles: #1.** GOLD **#2.** BORON **#3.**
IODINE **#4.** COBALT **#5.** OXYGEN **#6.**
HELIUM
Answer: NITROGEN

156. **Jumbles: #1.** OVEN **#2.** FOYER **#3.** ALARM
#4. CLOSET **#5.** SWITCH **#6.** CABINET
Answer: BASEMENT

157. **Jumbles: #1.** CAKE **#2.** CHEESE
#3. MUFFIN **#4.** WAFFLE **#5.** SPINACH
#6. PUDDING
Answer: SANDWICH
Quick Quiz Answer: PEACHES

158. **Jumbles: #1.** THUMB **#2.** SPLEEN
#3. THORAX **#4.** THYROID **#5.** STOMACH
#6. ABDOMEN
Answer: EARDRUM

159. **Jumbles: #1.** ERROR **#2.** BEACH
#3. TRIPLE **#4.** GOALIE **#5.** DEFENSE
#6. FAIRWAY
Answer: OFFENSE
Quick Quiz Answer: GOLF BALLS

160. **Jumbles: #1.** COSBY **#2.** HEE HAW
#3. RAWHIDE **#4.** MATLOCK **#5.** THE
SAINT **#6.** DEAR JOHN
Answer: BEWITCHED

161. **Jumbles: #1.** COMET **#2.** GALAXY
#3. URANUS **#4.** ECLIPSE **#5.** JUPITER
#6. NEPTUNE
Answer: SATURN

162. **Jumbles: #1.** FINCH **#2.** HYENA **#3.** LLAMA
#4. FERRET **#5.** BOBCAT **#6.** COUGAR
Answer: FLAMINGO

163. **Jumbles: #1.** SLOWLY **#2.** NOTICE
#3. REALIZE **#4.** BRAND **#5.** SECOND
#6. BECOMES
Answer: CALENDAR

164. **Jumbles: #1.** BOISE **#2.** AUSTIN
#3. LINCOLN **#4.** RALEIGH **#5.** OLYMPIA
#6. JACKSON
Answer: SACRAMENTO

165. **Jumbles: #1.** LOAN **#2.** MARK **#3.** VAULT
#4. STOCK **#5.** POUND **#6.** WALLET
Answer: DOLLAR

166. **Jumbles: #1.** ALICE **#2.** VEGAS **#3.** MAUDE
#4. DALLAS **#5.** CANNON **#6.** FLIPPER
Answer: PROVIDENCE

167. **Jumbles: #1.** KING **#2.** HULL **#3.** MARIS
#4. ERVING **#5.** JORDAN **#6.** MONTANA
Answer: JOE NAMATH

168. **Jumbles: #1.** PANDA **#2.** SKUNK
#3. BEAVER **#4.** CHICKEN **#5.** PANTHER
#6. PEACOCK
Answer: REINDEER

169. **Jumbles: #1.** BO DEREK **#2.** ROB REINER
#3. HUGH GRANT **#4.** KATHY BATES
#5. JANE CURTIN **#6.** WOODY ALLEN
Answer: BOB NEWHART

170. **Jumbles: #1.** ANKLE **#2.** TOOTH
#3. FEMUR **#4.** MOUTH **#5.** ARTERY
#6. THROAT
Answer: FOREARM

171. **Jumbles: #1.** CYPRUS **#2.** CORSICA
#3. ICELAND **#4.** JAMAICA **#5.** BAHAMAS
#6. BERMUDA
Answer: HISPANIOLA

172. **Jumbles: #1.** HIPPO **#2.** FINCH **#3.** LIZARD
#4. TURTLE **#5.** TURKEY **#6.** GIRAFFE
#7. CHICKEN
Answer: PANTHER
Quick Quiz Answer: ELEPHANT

173. **Jumbles: #1.** FREUD **#2.** GANDHI
#3. MOZART **#4.** LINCOLN **#5.** NAPOLEON
#6. COLUMBUS
Answer: COPERNICUS

174. **Jumbles: #1.** ROCKY **#2.** GANDHI
#3. PATTON **#4.** PLATOON **#5.** RAIN MAN
#6. THE STING
Answer: TITANIC

175. **Jumbles: #1.** MIAMI **#2.** OMAHA
#3. DALLAS **#4.** SEATTLE **#5.** ORLANDO
#6. MEMPHIS
Answer: DETROIT

176. **Jumbles: #1.** VOLGA **#2.** TIGRIS
#3. DANUBE **#4.** AMAZON **#5.** YANGTZE
#6. POTOMAC
Answer: COLUMBIA

177. **Jumbles: #1.** MINOR **#2.** TEMPO
#3. MELODY **#4.** RHYTHM **#5.** CANTATA
#6. ALLEGRO
Answer: HARMONY

Do You Know Any Kids?

If you'd like to see kids use their

RAISBN

to develop skills that could help them get ahead in

CSOLOH

then you should

NOSICERD

buying them **Jumble® BrainBusters Junior**. It's packed full of fun puzzles covering a wide range of subjects.

Call toll free 1-800-335-5323 to order your copy of **Jumble® BrainBusters Junior.**

U.S. STATE CAPITALS

JUMBLE BrainBusters! Junior

Unscramble the Jumbles, one letter to each square, to spell U.S. state capitals.

#1 EEHANL

#2 EUAJUN

#3 TATNAAL

#4 RENTONT

#5 PLYIAMO

Arrange the circled letters to solve the mystery answer.

MYSTERY ANSWER

Montgomery	Baton Rouge	Columbus
Juneau	Augusta	Oklahoma City
Phoenix	Annapolis	Salem
Little Rock	Boston	Harrisburg
Sacramento	Lansing	Providence
Denver	St. Paul	Columbia
Hartford	Jackson	Pierre
Dover	Jefferson City	Nashville
Tallahassee	Helena	Austin
Atlanta	Lincoln	Salt Lake City
Honolulu	Carson City	Montpelier
Boise	Concord	Richmond
Springfield	Trenton	Olympia
Indianapolis	Santa Fe	Charleston
Des Moines	Albany	Madison
Topeka	Raleigh	Cheyenne
Frankfort	Bismarck	

Box of Clues

Stumped? Maybe you can find a clue below.

-Georgia   -Hawaii
-Alaska   -Washington
-New Jersey -Montana